BOROUGH OF TWICK
LOCAL HISTORY SC

Paper Number 104

PICTURES OF HAMPTON
IN THE 1940s, 1950s & 1960s

THE ROADS AND BUILDINGS, BUSINESSES AND SHOPS, THE RIVER AND RECREATION

JOHN SHEAF

ISBN: 978-1-911145-04-2   Price £7.50

Dedication

This book is dedicated to Sharman, Richard, Thomas, Alice, Zoe and Ava and to all true Hamptonians, past, present and future.

~

A fervent wish is expressed to all readers of this book to do their best to preserve the history, artefacts and buildings of this ancient place.

Front Cover: The junction of Thames Street and Church Street (off to the right) looking past the old *Feathers Inn* (now divided into cottages numbered 2, 4 & 6 Thames Street) towards *The Bell* and the tower of St Mary's Church in 1965. Note the sign post to the M4 Motorway points towards Church Street as the M25 motorway did not exist at that time.

CONTENTS

INTRODUCTION

AS THE TITLE '*Pictures of Hampton in the 1940s, 1950s and 1960s*' implies this book is focused on images, particularly photographs, of Hampton during that war-time and post-war period.

An earlier book '*Images of Hampton in the 1920s and 1930s*' (BOTLHS Paper 100, 2017) concentrated on the roads of Hampton during the 1920s and 1930s and the changes that occurred during that time. It covered people at work, businesses and shops, how they developed and changes during that period. It also looked at people at play and a variety of popular recreational activities related to Hampton. This book takes that earlier work forward and looks at the same topics during the 1940s, 1950s and 1960s and, of course, includes a look at life in Hampton during the Second World War.

One reason to showcase these images is their comparative rarity and consequent lack of usage in other publications. Ironically images from an earlier period, the Edwardian era, leading up towards the First World War are much more common. This was because picture postcards were then widely collected and many were saved in albums. The contents of many of these albums have survived until the present day and are thus more readily available to be collected and used to illustrate books. Later, in the 1920s and 1930s, after the First World War, the nation was in a far less frivolous mood than in the 'endless summers' before the Great War and collecting postcards was much less popular. Their use was also declining due to the rise of the telephone, improving transport links and eventually increasing car usage, as well as the rising cost of postage. Overall there were fewer postcards being used and far, far fewer people collecting them and thus preserving them for future generations. It was also still fairly early days in terms of amateur photography and when photographs were taken they were frequently not titled or identified and within a generation or two were forgotten - and in many cases thrown away as well.

During the Second World War years there are not large numbers of local photographs. This is mainly due to photographic film being unobtainable for civilian use and, in any case, the use of a camera would have attracted the attention of the police or military authorities. The occasional photo does exist; some are official photos, some may have been taken using supplies of pre-war film and there was also the odd amount of "leakage" from workplaces that had access to film, eg the NPL at Teddington. In the aftermath of the war, photos were still relatively scarce. Additionally, many amateur photographers did not label their photographs and so albums of pictures may have been unwittingly disposed of or, if they survive, are unrecognised and so not available to use as illustrations. Fortunately, the Hampton Research Group (of the Borough of Twickenham Local History Society which had been formed in 1962) was fairly assiduous in taking photographs of the locality and we have been able to utilise a good number of these images. In terms of postcards there are not a great number as the heyday of collecting postcards was long since over and not many local cards were produced except those covering holiday destinations and visitor attractions.

Finally, we have been able to call upon some images from '*The Borough Plans*'. These images are now available to search online at: https://richmond.spydus.co.uk/cgi-bin/spydus.exe/MSGTRN/OPAC/ARC?HOMEPRMS=ARCPARAMS

[In order to access these plans go to the Advanced Search tab and enter "PLA/*" in the 'Reference Number' field as well as any other search criteria, eg a road name in the 'Anywhere' field.]

This website includes thousands of original plans for housing of the Borough, many beautifully drawn and coloured. These also help us to capture some of the excitement of a new post WW2 era here.

MAP 1

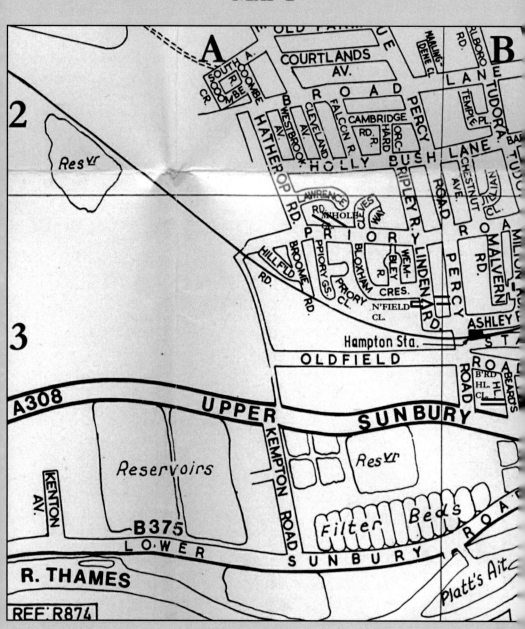

Hampton South West

Map 2

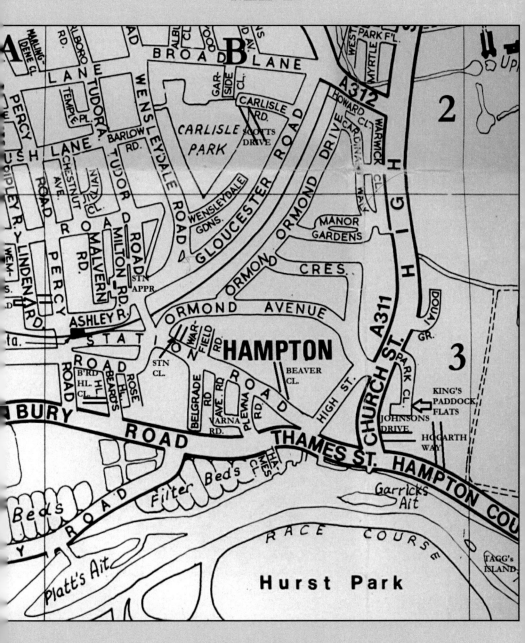

Hampton South East

MAP 3

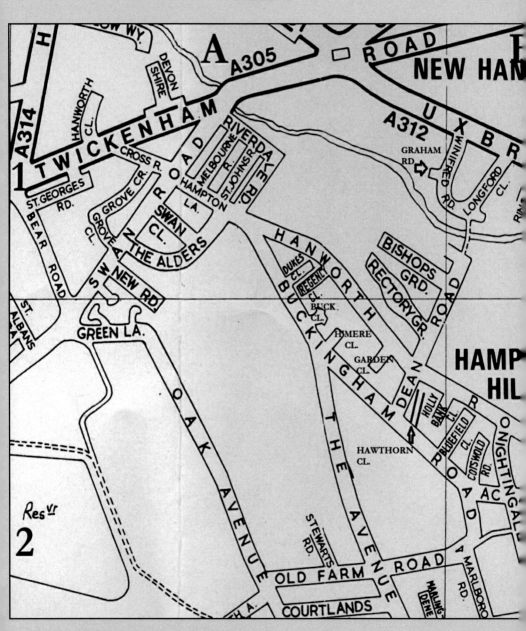

Hampton North West

MAP 4

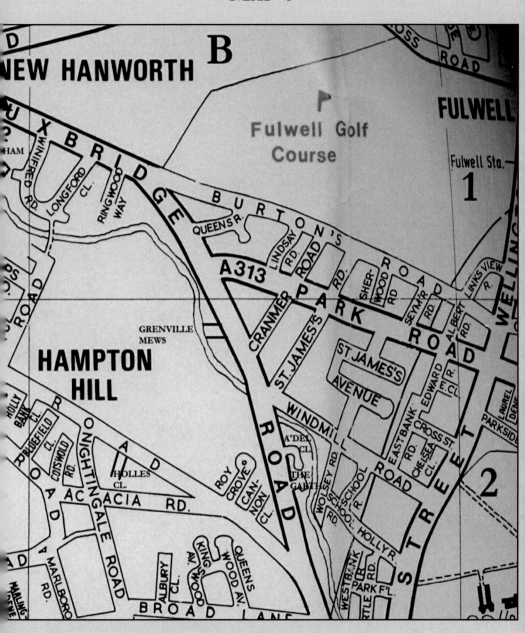

Hampton North East

HAMPTON IN THE 1940s, 1950s & 1960s

The 1940s

THE SECOND WORLD War dominated the first half of the 1940s and indeed its impact had been felt well before, and was still very evident, long after those years. As early as September 1935, Air Raid Precautions (ARP) had been brought to the attention of Hampton UDC when the County Council wrote to them re-formulating a scheme for Air Raid Precautions (*Thames Valley Times*, 11 September 1935). There was a Public Meeting on the subject held in the Public Hall, Church Street, Hampton on 30 November 1936. A poster notes that this was to *"enlist the interest and assistance of the Public in making provision for the protection of the lives and limbs of themselves and their families in the event of any future attack from the air by enemy air-craft"*. Other planning included the recruitment of large numbers of ARP wardens and the setting up of wardens' posts as well as establishing rescue parties. One was based at the Council Depot at the corner of Oldfield Road and Rosehill (until recently largely occupied by the Postal Sorting Office), with numerous other groupings to carry out a huge variety of tasks.

In any event the war had started, a few months before the period covered by this book, on 3 September 1939 and ended, in Europe, on 8 May 1945. That year, though, did not mark the end of the effects of the war. The huge number of deaths, injuries and destruction had the most enormous impact, both at home and abroad, that lasted for very many years. Aside from that, on a purely practical day-to-day basis, was the impact of rationing which was also to last for many years. In all, food rationing lasted for 14 years and did not finally end until July 1954.

As soon as the war started the effects on local schooling were apparent. Percy Road Council School (now Hampton Juniors) was largely taken over for use as a First Aid Post, Ambulance Depot, and Air Raid Wardens' Post although some classes continued there for girls for some of the wartime. Fortuitously, Hampton Grammar School (now Hampton School) had moved to a new site in the Hanworth Road in 1939 and, as such, the former premises on the Upper Sunbury Road were empty. This enabled the boys to spend the war at the old Grammar School premises and the girls to spend a large part of the war there. (Before the war boys and girls were educated at the Percy Road premises on separate floors of the building and had a separate Headmaster and Headmistress.)

As far as practical preparations in the event of aerial bombardment were concerned, there was a distribution of Anderson shelters in the Borough. (These shelters, designed to accommodate up to six people, were built of galvanised, corrugated, steel panels, curved at the top, and buried 4 ft (1.2 metres) deep in the soil and then covered with a minimum of 15 inches (38 cm) of soil above the roof). (NB Hampton and other areas had become part of the enlarged Borough of Twickenham in 1937.) By May 1940 almost all the shelters needed in the Borough had been delivered. There were also public shelters, including surface shelters and basements and, for example, there was a large public shelter in Manor Gardens dug under the large grassed traffic island in that road.

The first bomb to fall on the Borough fell on Hampton on 24 August 1940 on a house in Tudor Road. Bombing was sustained for most of the rest of 1940 and then there was mainly a lull in this area, until the "Little Blitz" at the beginning of 1944. A Hampton resident, Mary Grimes of 72 High Street, recorded in her diary: "*Sunday 3 November 1940 First night without Raid for 50 NIGHTS. A German plane was over in afternoon and machine gunned and was shot at*". In this period there were obviously some very heavy raids on Hampton on some occasions, eg: "*Thursday 26 September 1940 Bombs in Thames Street, Plevna, Ormond. Tops off pinnacle of Church. Station Road Allens*". Another particular occasion is recorded as: *"Friday 11 October 1940 Tremendous bombing in night of Friday. Row of shops and houses down, Percy Tuffin's etc, like earthquake"* (This refers to the high explosive bomb that destroyed the properties mentioned in the Station Road part of the 'Main Roads' section of the book).

Back at Percy Road School (at this time relocated to the old Grammar School site) the effects were also being felt as these entries from the School Log Book record: *"20 September 1940 Nearly the whole of Monday was spent in the shelters owing to air raids, the last one continuing until 6pm. Two girls have this week left the School one girl having been evacuated to Australia whilst another has had her house bombed and is now staying with relatives in Huntingdon."* Another entry notes: *"4 November 1940 The School was closed by order of the Police owing to an unexploded bomb falling in the playground on the evening of 15 October. A week's holiday was granted for the mid-term. The Royal Engineers spent two days here in order to extract the bomb but it cannot be found."* Shortages were also having an impact: *"21 April 1941 A new type of slate, rubber and pencil has been received for each child, in order to save exercise paper."*

There were impacts, of course, on the non-school population as these extracts, from letters written by Mrs Faith Buckley of Carlisle Road, Hampton, to her daughters who had been evacuated to Toronto, Canada, record. *"27 June 1940 Windows. We are protecting ours from "blast" as we should hate to sit all winter with cardboard or wood shuttered windows! The back of the house has butter muslin stuck on all the windows with paste - very bridal looking but not very transparent. The front is covered with a sort of transparent veneer but it spoils one's outlook."*

She then records some of the practical steps people were taking towards the war effort. *"I have been arranging to have a salvage depot for the next two weeks. I have arranged for Mr Stevens in the High Street to lend me his shop. People will bring in all their old aluminium, brass, copper etc. and we encourage them to turn out their lofts, cupboards, garages etc. and it all goes to help with the war by turning it into ammunition. We even have boxes for old razor blades, nails, keys etc. It will be manned by different people taking turns to be at the shop to receive the things."*

Some of the less obvious hazards of the war are also apparent when she writes: *"25 March 1941 I am sending you three pieces of shell splinters. The long narrow one came down in the garden and the other two in the side passage. I was wondering if you would like to let your friends (and teachers) hold and examine them. Perhaps you could charge 1 cent towards your efforts for helping the war. They are pieces of our own shells fired from anti-aircraft guns during raids and a few moments after the shell goes up you hear this stuff falling around. The copper piece smashed a tile on our roof and brought it crashing to the ground. It is because of this stuff that people do not like going out in a raid without a tin helmet."*

War time shortages are very apparent in this list that she writes in another letter:

"11 November 1941

Dear, it is all very well to say buy Father a fountain pen but they are - like many other things - off the market at the moment. Here is a list of some of the things I go to buy and am told "oh no we cannot get those now":

bicycle pumps	*kirby hair grips*	*tooth paste*	*pearl buttons*
fountain pens	*hair pins and nets*	*sweets*	*darning wool*
nail varnish	*face cream*	*soap flakes*	*jellies*
ginger	*tools*	*nails*	*cornflakes*
rice krispies	*brown paper*	*paint boxes*	*sponges"*

The fact of so many men being away fighting had its impact at home in many ways as this extract notes: *"3 February 1942.... For instance we have been asked to provide as many toys and as much furniture as possible for day nurseries being opened in Twickenham Borough. A Day Nursery is where a Mother can leave her children for a shilling a day while she does war work. She can leave them from 7am to 9pm and they are fed and looked after until collected. There is a great demand for them because women are now doing all sorts of jobs, milk and baker rounds, conductresses on trolley buses and buses, postwomen as well as factory workers."*

Efforts to combat various shortages and to 'grow your own' are apparent in these extracts: *"September 6th 1942 There are dustbins all along the pavements painted white and marked PIG FOOD and we all take our bits and pieces and dump them in the bin and the pig cart comes and collects it three times a week. One wanders down the road with a colander or sink basket full of potato peelings, apple peel or stale bread etc and there at the pig bin you meet your neighbours, lift the lid, dump your bits and bobs…….. There is a big shortage of paper here. We take all our paper bags back to the shops. You see signs " Bring your own Paper" or " Biscuits and eggs only supplied if you bring your own bag". "Bring your own dish and save paper".*

As noted earlier, after the terrible bombing of 1940 there was mainly a lull in aerial bombardment in this area until 1944 when the Luftwaffe *"managed to assemble a force of over 500 aircraft in Northern France"*. The attacks that followed impacted on the Borough and on Hampton until the final attack by conventional bombing in this phase of the war on the night of 14 March. Our diarist, Mary Grimes, at 72 High Street, Hampton recorded (rather briefly and seemingly rather nonchalantly!): *"21 January 1944 SHELL KNOCKED MY HOUSE OUT, not hurt me, went to Billy's at 5.30 am (Sat) back home by 10 am."*

A newspaper cutting, stuck into her diary gives rather more detail: *"Two A.A. Shells fell in Hampton on Saturday morning, causing slight damage to two doors in the Police Station yard and to the house at 72 High Street. The shell which fell on the private house went through the roof, fell into the bedroom, exploded and damaged the walls and then penetrated the bedroom floor and finished up on the ground floor, after passing through an armchair. A woman alone in the house who was sheltering under the stairs was unhurt."*

The summer of 1944 saw the beginning of the attack on this country by the new German secret weapons the V1 and V2. The V1s were the cruise missiles of their time and had a top speed of 400 mph and flew at 2000 to 3000 ft. Very fortunately only 27 landed in the Borough but a number of people were killed including an old lady in Longford Close, Hampton, and others were injured in other incidents. By a stroke of luck, we have a first-hand report of the sighting of a V1 above Hampton which very fortunately did not land here. The recollection is by Raymond Manning who, between 1941-1945, lived at *Orme House* (4 Church Street) which despite being a rather grand house was being used as a small 'shadow factory' for the war effort at the time. The firm occupying the house had been bombed out of the St Paul's area of London on 29 December 1940 and moved to Hampton. Raymond's parents were employed as caretaker and cook (for about 15 people) in the house.

Raymond recalls: *"I well remember one early evening (after my father's death) when I was in the house with just my mother and I was drawing in the kitchen, when my mother (who was very hard of hearing) said she would take a bath in the third floor bathroom at the back of the house. She had been gone about 10 minutes when I was shocked to hear the bell ring. Now this bell could only give about two minutes or so warning as buzz bombs could speed at over 350mph and I knew my mother would not hear it! I also knew she was very vulnerable – high up and facing the flight path. Anyway, not knowing quite what to do I charged up several flights of stairs and when I reached the landing windows I heard the bomb coming so I knew there was nothing I could do for my mother or myself. So, thus resigned, I calmly pulled aside the net curtains (net curtains were obligatory in the terms of Mr Knight's tenancy contract) and looked out of the window which gave a clear view over Bushy Park. Then I saw the bomb coming straight overhead, the engine noise was terrific and all the old sash windows were rattling, but somehow*

I wasn't afraid. Then, when the bomb was almost overhead the engine cut out! Fortunately, it didn't nose-dive, as most did, but glided on to impact in Sunbury. I had rushed to the front windows and saw the great plume of black smoke arise in the sky. By this time in the war, I was, like most others, inured to bombs, so I calmly went down to the kitchen and carried on drawing. Ten minutes later my mother entered the room saying "I think we'll have a cup of tea", being totally oblivious of the drama just played out, and I never did tell her."

Later, a total of 1200 of the technically more sophisticated V2s were aimed at London but only one fell on the Borough and that was in Teddington and so Hampton escaped those rockets which had a top speed of 3500 mph. Not long after, in May 1945, the country celebrated VE Day and then the end of the war in August 1945. The official London Victory Celebrations were not held until June 1946 (see the 'People at Play - Recreation and Celebration' section for a description of these celebrations).

At the end of hostilities there was a need to address the local housing issues. Obviously, a number of homes had been destroyed in the bombing, others were so badly damaged that they had to be pulled down and rebuilt and even more were so badly damaged that they had been evacuated but could be repaired. In addition, a very large number were slightly damaged. Work started on this rebuilding and repair although it took many years to complete. As an example, the house of Mary Grimes that had been bombed in 1944, at 72 High Street, was not finally repaired until the middle of 1951.

The Borough organised an exhibition at York House in Twickenham, held from 11-22 March 1946, in order to come up with plans and solutions to the housing crisis and to obtain public feedback. A brochure accompanying the exhibition lists various actions to be taken. These included "Immediate relief" – taking over empty houses and by erecting emergency unwanted army Nissen Huts (not intended for occupation for more than two years), "The short-term housing programme" – accepting from the Ministry prefabricated bungalows (intended to remain for 10 years), and "Long term policy" – the building of permanent houses on a large scale. It goes on to say that the only extensive areas of unbuilt land in the Borough are amenity open spaces and the market garden area at Hampton. To build on the former, it notes, would destroy the amenities and to build on the market gardens would destroy a useful local industry supplying food to a large region and was anyway prohibited by the Government in the interests of the general regional plan. In the meantime, it also stated, the Borough was building on such limited sites as were available.

In Hampton, a site for "Temporary Bungalows" (pre-fabs) had been identified in Oldfield Road and 13 were proposed for the site which was along the edge of the former Grammar School playing fields in that road. As far as permanent houses were concerned sites had been identified at Fairlight, the site of a large house at the junction of Uxbridge Road and Windmill Road (although this was not actually built on until 1963), further houses in Uxbridge Road, and also an extension to the Longford Estate, off the Uxbridge Road. And so, despite the best of intentions, it took a long time for significant new roads to be developed (see the 'New Roads' section for further information).

The 1950s

At the beginning of the 1950s the country was still in the grip of post-war rationing that was not destined to end until 1954. The government was trying to promote a feeling of recovery from the devastation of the war and so the Festival of Britain had been held in 1951. Shortly afterwards King George VI died and Queen Elizabeth II became the new monarch on 6 February 1952 and was crowned the following year. (see the 'People at Play - Recreation and Celebration' section for description of the local impact of these celebrations).

This sense of renewal began to help lift the national mood. However, apart from post-war rebuilding and repair in Hampton there was still little in the way of new roads being built probably due in part to lack of available land as well as shortages of material. In fact, in the first half of the 1950s, only one new road, Thames Close, was constructed and it was built by the Metropolitan Water Board (MWB) on their own land, and not by the Council, as housing for employees. However, construction was to pick up later and in the end a total of ten new roads were constructed during the decade as well as building on various other plots, some not without controversy.

These were very different times of course and there was less awareness of the desirability of preserving heritage. Also, Councillors in those days, once elected, saw little need to consult residents any further and governed as they thought fit. This was to lead to sustained areas of disagreement especially once the Hampton Residents Association (now Hampton Society) was formed in 1956. In fact, the Association was formed primarily to object to a planning application to convert *Grove House* (100 High Street) to offices and to build housing in the large grounds.

In the end many of the proposed housing schemes were built although in many cases in a much less damaging way than the original proposals. In the case of *Grove House*, the house was converted to offices (but without any substantial change to the external appearance) and the houses of Douai Grove constructed on a large portion of the rear garden. However, a later proposal to demolish the house altogether and construct new houses was rejected. Ironically, in recent years *Grove House* has now been converted back from offices to a house.

Some smaller sites were not so fortunate and Thames Street lost two groups of picturesque old cottages and Station Road another group of cottages despite much protest. (See the section 'Main Roads' for details of these and other proposed changes).

The 1960s

In this decade house building picked up considerably and a total of 27 new roads were built in Hampton. Not only was demand still high but, at last, some of the land of former nurseries was starting to become available. As was noted earlier the Council recognised immediately after the war, that this was effectively the only large area of land potentially available for housing in the whole Borough but, at the time, it was still required for food production. Many of the nurseries were significant innovators and constantly tried to improve their methods and yields. However, particularly from the 1960s onwards, air freight became cheaper and it became viable to import products from more far flung places which had much cheaper labour costs and warmer climates and could thus undercut what could be produced in Hampton. Gradually individual nurseries began to disappear and make way for housing development. (See the section 'New Roads' for further information). Of course, the main area of former nurseries in the north west of Hampton (now known as the Nurserylands) went on to survive a little longer before becoming derelict and finally being built on in the late 1970s and 1980s.

Other changes occurred in the 1960s including the closure of the Hurst Park race course on Molesey Hurst on the Molesey side of the river in 1962 with its knock-on effect on Hampton Ferry (see the 'People at Play' section for further information on the ferry). A new Methodist Church was built in Percy Road, in front of the earlier building, and was dedicated on 9 November 1963. The old Public Hall, in Church Street, was demolished in the mid-1960s and replaced by a new Parish Hall, the present Community Hall, in 1968. When the old hall was demolished the Borough of Twickenham Local History Society (BOTLHS) conducted an archaeological "dig". It was hoped that the site of the dig, near the church and the vicarage, might reveal traces of the old tithe barn but in the event nothing of any great significance was discovered. Another local facility, the much-loved Bearsted Maternity Hospital, housed in what is now known as Rotary Court in Hampton Court Road, where many from Hampton had been born, was lost when it closed in 1969 despite a petition with more than 8000 signatures.

In 1969 two new schools were opened in Hampton: Hampton Infant School and Clarendon School. The new infants' school in Ripley Road was built on the site of a former nursery. The school had previously been located in Station Road since 1874 (originally as a girls' and infants' school). The girls moved out in 1907, to the then new Percy Road Council School (now Hampton Juniors), and the infants remained at the Station Road Infants' School until 1969 when the new school was built in Ripley Road. The old school was demolished in 1971 and the site is now occupied by a block of maisonettes called Rushbury Court. Clarendon School, a special school, opened in Hanworth Road in 1969 and remained there until 2018 when the primary school moved to Buckingham Road, Hampton, and the secondary school moved to Egerton Road, Twickenham.

AIR RAID PRECAUTIONS.

A

Public Meeting

will be held at

THE PUBLIC HALL,

CHURCH STREET, HAMPTON,

on

Monday, 30th November, 1936,

at 8 p.m.

in order to enlist the interest and assistance of the Public in making provision for the protection of the lives and limbs of themselves and their families in the event of any future attack from the air by enemy air-craft.

The Meeting will be addressed and the objects explained by

Wing-Commander A. Steele-Perkins, O.B.E.

OF THE HOME OFFICE,

and by

C. le Strange Metcalfe, Esq.,

of the British Red Cross Society.

EDGAR COZENS,

Clerk to the Hampton Urban District Council.

Left: 1936 Poster for an Air Raid Precautions meeting to make provision for protection "*in the event of any future attack from the air by enemy air-craft.*"

Right: A Borough of Twickenham Light Rescue Party vehicle, and the members of the crew, which was based at the Council Depot at the corner of Oldfield Road and Rosehill.

Below: Girls from Percy Road Council School (now Hampton Juniors) were evacuated to the old Grammar School in Upper Sunbury Road and are seen here in 1942 with their teacher Mrs J C Quantrill.

Left: A bombed house in Tudor Avenue on 24 August 1940.

Below: Broken chimney pots and other debris in front of the air raid shelter which was flooded after the water main burst during the bombing of 24 August 1940 in Tudor Avenue.

Above: The 10th Platoon, 9th Middlesex Battalion, Home Guard. (Hampton Launch Works Defence Group, 6 July 1941) outside the Thornycroft offices on Platts Eyot.

Below: The 10th Platoon, 9th Middlesex Battalion, Home Guard. 'B' Section firing instructions on Platts Eyot.

Above: The 10th Platoon, 9th Middlesex Battalion, Home Guard. 'A' Section grenade throwing on Platts Eyot.

Christmas
Greetings

1946

Left: A homemade Hampton Christmas card for 1946, when there was still a shortage of many items and materials, showing the riverside, *The Bell* and St Mary's Church.

Above: These German POWs were still working at the nursery of K E Page, Oak Avenue, Hampton in 1947 where they are standing in front of a heap of coal for the boiler.

Below: One of the pre-fabricated bungalows in Oldfield Road, on the edge of the old Grammar School playing fields, built c1945 and photographed in 1955.

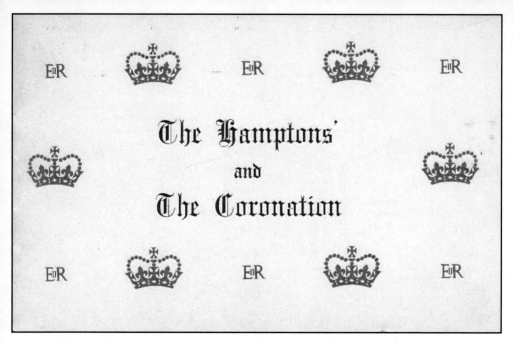

Above: The cover of an information booklet produced for the 1953 Coronation.

Below: Site plan for houses built in Thames Close, off Thames Street, in 1952 to house workers of the Metropolitan Water Board.

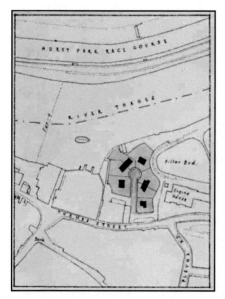

Page opposite, above: Grove House at 100 High Street and its proposed redevelopment was the main reason for the setting up of the Hampton Residents Association (now Hampton Society) in 1956.

Page opposite, below: One of several groups of cottages, these in Thames Street next to the old Fire Station, that were lost to redevelopment in the 1950s.

Left: The Hurst Park race course closed in October 1962 and this was a major loss of business to Hampton Ferry run by George Kenton.

Mr. George Kenton, the Hampton ferry keeper, and the men who helped him run the race-day ferries to Hurst Park, from the left, Messrs. C. Baker, C. Glazier, P. Heath and W. Major.

Left: A leaflet for the 1963 dedication of the new Methodist Church in Percy Road.

Page opposite, above: The old Public Hall, looking down Church Street, in a view towards The Studio and the Riverside.

Page opposite, below: After demolition of the old Public Hall the Borough of Twickenham Local History Society (BOTLHS) carried out a 'dig' in 1967 but little of substance was found.

Above: Some of the dignitaries, including the mayor and mayoress, at the opening of Clarendon School in Hanworth Road in May 1969.

Page opposite, above: A petition to save the Bearsted Memorial Hospital in Hampton Court Road (now Rotary Court) being signed outside the chemist's shop in Station Approach in 1968.

Page opposite, below: Hampton Infants' School in Ripley Road under construction in January 1969.

MAIN ROADS

INCLUDED IN THIS section are the important roads of Hampton. These are Church Street, Hampton Court Road, High Street, Station Road, Thames Street, Upper Sunbury Road and Uxbridge Road. These are mainly ancient through roads dating back several centuries, although the Uxbridge Road came into being as a result of the 1826 Enclosure. Their history has been described in *"The Highways and Byways of Hampton – A short history of every street in Hampton"* (BOTLHS Paper 88, 2009) and more recently there was a description of the roads and buildings in 1911-1912 in *"Hampton 100 years ago"* (BOTLHS Paper 95, 2015). Another book, *"Images of Hampton in the 1920s and 1930s"* (BOTLHS Paper 100, 2017), covered the period of the 1920s and 1930s where each of the main roads had a separate section which describes the main changes that occurred in each of them during that time period. This book follows on from that period and does the same thing for the period of the 1940s, 1950s and 1960s.

There is a close-up map for each of these roads. The most up to date map at around the start of our time period – the war time 1941 ARP Provisional edition, 5 inch map – has been used for all of the main roads except for the Uxbridge Road which does not appear on the original. For that road only the 1939 Provisional edition, 6 inch map has been used.

The text for each road outlines the significant changes that occurred during our time period and this is followed by a number of illustrations showing how the road looked in the 1940s, 1950s and 1960s.

CHURCH STREET

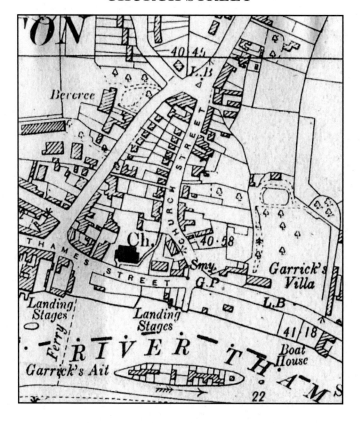

Church Street is one of the ancient roads of Hampton and was well defined by the 17ᵗʰ Century. In the 1940s, 1950s and 1960s, the time frame covered by this book, there was not a great deal of change until several things happened in the late 1960s.

On the eastern side of the street a new turning, Johnsons Drive, was built near the junction with Hampton Court Road. It is first recorded on the 1969 Register of Electors and was built on part of the Garrick's Villa estate (see the section 'New Roads' for further information).

Further up the road, on the eastern side, Nos 20-24 had been occupied in the 1940 directory by the Hampton-on-Thames Laundry

Ltd, later known as The Hampton Laundry Ltd. The laundry disappeared in around the late 1960s and the premises became a warehouse and subsequently a builder's yard and was later converted to offices (now occupied by Petrovalves).

The most noticeable change was on the western side of the road on the site of what is now the Community Hall. When the old St Mary's Church was rebuilt in 1830-31 a new school, on the site of the modern Community Hall in Church Street, was built and opened in 1834. The north end housed the Grammar or Upper 'Department or School' and the south end was utilised by the English or Lower. The schools gradually became more separated and in 1880 the Grammar School moved to new premises in Upper Sunbury Road. The English School remained until 1907 when Percy Road Council School (now Hampton Juniors) was built. The former school building in Church Street was then converted to a Public Hall. It was demolished in the mid-1960s and replaced by a new Parish Hall, the present Community Hall, in 1968.

Further up the western side of Church Street is the old Wesleyan Chapel. This had been built in 1861 and stayed in use as a Chapel until 1926 when a new building, in Percy Road, now the Methodist Church, was opened. The building then had various uses in our time frame, including being used as a cold store and, after the war, for half a century as an Electric Blanket Repair Centre. After that it fell into serious decay before being renovated in recent years for housing use.

Still on the western side of the road the shop at No 33 was run by Thomas J Leggett, newsagent, confectioner and tobacconist and was called Leggett's, under subsequent owners, throughout our time period. These premises were extensively renovated and converted into two houses (33 and 35 Church Street) in 1999.

CHURCH ST HAMPTON 3.

Above: The southern end of Church Street, at the junction with Thames Street, looking past 'The Studio' at No 1 towards the old Public Hall in the 1950s.

Below: A laundry box from The Hampton Laundry Ltd at 20-24 Church Street dating from 1962.

Please Return Boxes Regularly

THE HAMPTON LAUNDRY L™.

CHURCH STREET

HAMPTON   MIDDLESEX

12 62

Above: The old Public Hall in 1963 in a view looking north.

A NEW HALL FOR HAMPTON !

Artist's impression of the proposed new hall
{Plan on back page}

Left: A fund raising brochure for the new Parish Hall (now the Community Hall).

Right: The old Wesleyan Chapel had become an Electric Blanket Repair Centre by the time of this 1963 image and is now converted to residential use.

Below: The northern end of Church Street, at The Triangle, with the old *White Hart* to the left and the junction with High Street on the right.

HAMPTON COURT ROAD

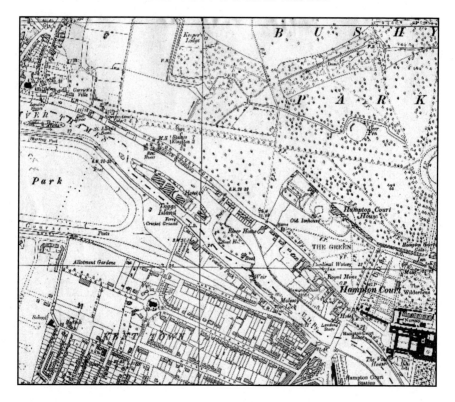

Hampton Court Road is part of an ancient through road known as 'The Windsor to Kingston Road' (now part of the A308). It contains some very old buildings particularly those opposite Hampton Court Green.

The 1940s, 1950s and 1960s saw some changes and additional buildings. One of these was a block of flats called Brunstan Court on land belonging to a very large house called *River Home*, opposite the present car park at the end of Hampton Court Green. *River Home* itself survived until the 1970s and its former boat house (often called the Swiss Chalet or Hucks Boatyard) is extant. Most of the land that went with the house was developed in the early 1930s after a planning application for 16 detached houses was submitted in December 1929. At least two of these houses, *Deepwater* and

Tamesis, were rebuilt in 1947 after war damage. Another property on this land, formerly a trolleybus electricity sub-station, was converted into a house called *Torrent House,* in 1962.

During the war a temporary bridge was built from Hampton Court Road to connect with Taggs Island. In 1941 A.C. Cars had purchased the freehold of the island, still then owned by the Kent family who had leased it to Tom Tagg nearly a century before. The magnificent skating rink and covered tennis courts of the entertainment complex and hotel that had previously been known successively as the Karsino, the Thames Riviera, the Palm Beach and the Casino Hotel were converted to a munitions factory. A bridge was then built to connect the island to the riverside to move materials and manufactured goods back and forth. This Bailey bridge (a portable, pre-fabricated truss bridge which was meant to be removed at the end of the war) collapsed in 1965 and was reinstated before a new permanent bridge was built in 1982.

Further westwards *St Albans* stood on the Hampton Court Road, almost opposite the *White Lodge* in Bushy Park Stockyard. It was a very large, much extended, four-storey house and stood throughout our time frame but disappeared very shortly afterwards. In addition, there was a separate stable building (with seven stalls) with staff accommodation above, which is now known as *St Albans Lodge*.

The owners of *St Albans*, Winifred Graham (Mrs Cory) died in 1950 and Theodore Cory in 1961. In order that the house might be preserved as a memorial to Winifred Graham, Theodore Cory had bequeathed *St Albans* to the Borough of Twickenham in 1961. His will stated that the bequest should be used as a Museum for the benefit of the inhabitants of Hampton. After years of prevarication and legal wrangling the Council (which had accepted the gift in 1954) let matters drift for so long that the house became ever more dilapidated and many of the fixture and fittings were stolen.

On 24 February 1972 the Council attached a notice to the door of *St Albans* saying that there would be three weeks to protest against demolition. The following day, demolition started; the Council claimed the building was dangerous (having itself prevaricated for 11 years). This brought an end to this large riverside house which had stood beside the Thames at Hampton for nearly 300 years.

Somewhat ironically *St Albans Lodge*, which had originally been stables with staff accommodation above, survived.

The fate of *St Albans Lodge* was also subject to protracted wrangling. It is now split into three apartments. The only visible remains of the main house are a flat grass area, where the house once

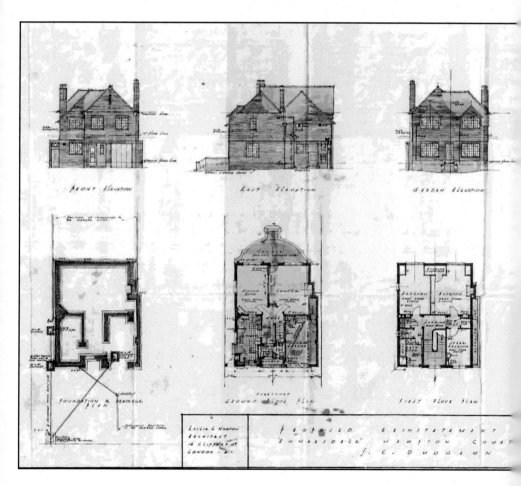

stood, and a large cedar tree that stood next to the house. The former garden of *St Albans* is however, fortunately, a public open space beside the river *"for the benefit of the inhabitants of Hampton"*, and as a lasting memorial to the former inhabitants of *St Albans*.

Below: 'Proposed reinstatement' plans, after war damage, of *Ennersdale* now *Deepwater* in Hampton Court Road, dated 1947.

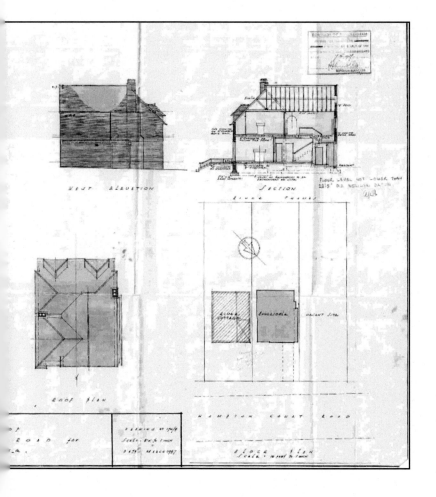

Above: A 667 trolleybus passing the entrance approach to the Casino Hotel on Taggs Island with the Swiss Chalet (Huck's boatyard) behind.

Below: The collapsed Taggs Island bailey bridge in December 1965 was later reinstated and then rebuilt in 1982.

BRIDGE
UNSAFE
CLOSED TO
ALL
TRAFFIC

INCLUDING
PEDESTRIAN

Right: Garrick's Temple beside Hampton Court Road in 1966.

Right: Garrick's Villa on the opposite side of the road to the temple in 1966.

Above: St Albans in Hampton Court Road was left to the Borough as a museum but due to prevarication and legal wrangling this did not come about and it was demolished in 1972.

HIGH STREET

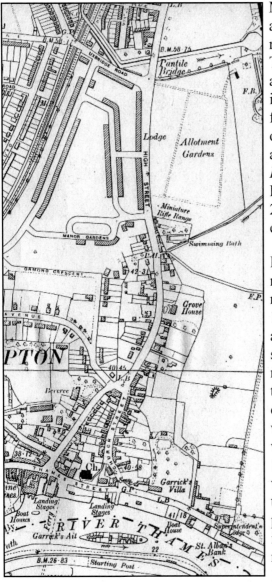

Modern High Street was another ancient through road, running towards Twickenham, which had a number of names and indeed different names for different parts of it over the centuries. (See also 'The Highways and Byways of Hampton', BOTLHS Paper 88, 2009, for a much fuller explanation).

Inevitably, in such a long road, there were a number of changes in the 1940s, 1950s and 1960s and these are summarised here. This is not straightforward as the last reliable street directory for Hampton was 1940 although there was a less reliable one in 1953. This means that we know the occupiers at the beginning of our time period in 1940 but there is no street directory to refer to for the end of the 1960s. Nevertheless, by looking at other publications, adverts and other items we can glean some idea of the occupiers for many, if not all, of the shops and businesses at various points in our time frame.

Firstly, we follow the western side of the road. *The Red Lion* at No 1 stayed the same throughout and Kingsbury's at No 3 stayed the same for much of the time, using it mainly for tyre storage, although it is recorded as a lampshade supplies business by 1969. No 5 was a grocers throughout starting as Madeley's and being occupied by Edwards from at least as early as 1953. Crossing Station Road and past Barclays bank the 1940 directory had a jeweller, tailor, fishmonger, boot maker, confectioner and printer before reaching *Castle House*. *Castle House* and its grounds had become mainly occupied by a timber merchants and saw mill in the 1930s with the house converted to offices for the company. By the end of our time period the jeweller had been K & N Press since at least 1953, the fate of the tailor is not clear and the fishmonger premises had housed various businesses as had the bootmaker. The confectioner had become the Box café by 1953 and continued as such into the 1980s; the printer is not identified. *Castle House* was still used by Hampton Timber Co until c1960 when the house was demolished and an industrial works built. There was a severe fire there in 1964 and the factory was rebuilt and occupied by a firm named Saft for many years. There was another major fire in 1984 and three quarters of the premises were damaged. The premises were rebuilt and the firm of Saft later closed down c1999. In 1990 new buildings were built as "live/work" spaces and some buildings were converted into offices and are now known as "Castle Business Village" recalling the name of *Castle House*. Next, Boyall's, an ironmonger, was there throughout as was Budd, radio and electrical, next door. Both premises were converted to flats in 2001. Captain Christie Crawfurd was still at *Beveree* in 1940 having moved there in 1891 but he died in 1948. After he died the house became a retirement home and since 1992 has been home to the Twickenham Preparatory School. The Council bought the 8.1 acre grounds from the estate for sporting and recreational purposes. Initially the football ground was used by Twickenham AFC and from 1959 by Hampton FC (now Hampton and Richmond Borough FC).

Continuing up the road, by far the largest change, starting a few years before the war, had been to the *Manor House* and *Manor*

House Farm. From the mid-1930s onwards this had become the Manor House Estate or Jubilee Estate, as it was first known after the 1935 Silver Jubilee of George V. This involved a number of new roads and, somewhat hidden by a large hedge between Warwick Close and the High Street, building was still continuing after the war in Manor Gardens, Cardinals Walk, Ormond Crescent and Ormond Drive.

We now return to the bottom end of High Street, near the junction with Thames Street, and follow the eastern side of the road. In 1940 the shops and pubs at this end of the street included a cafe, a tobacconist and confectioner, *The Jolly Gardeners*, a chemist, a fruiterer and a grocers, *The Jolly Coopers*, and a butchers. By c1969 these were still a cafe, a tobacconist and confectioner although *The Jolly Gardeners* had closed in 1955 and, still owned by the Heath family who had run the pub, had become CP Heath the boat builder. The chemist, fruiterer and grocers, *The Jolly Coopers*, and butchers had all stayed in the same use throughout the period. *The Jolly Coopers* still trades today and the café is now the Riverside, an Indian restaurant, but all the other premises have now been converted to housing.

At The Triangle the premises in 1940 were used as a coal merchants, a sports outfitters and a fruiterer and greengrocers. The coal merchants lasted at least into the 1960s and the sports outfitters at least until the 1950s. The fruiterer and greengrocers lasted into the 1990s and all are now converted to housing usage.

Going northwards from The Triangle the premises at 80a High Street was a tea room in 1940 but had become a ladies hairdressers by the 1960s and stayed as such at least until the 1980s although it is now converted to housing. Similarly, the shop at 116, F W Smith, a grocer was there until at least the 1950s but is also now converted to a house. Between these two addresses a new turning, Douai Grove, is first recorded on the 1958 Register of Electors (see the 'New Roads' section for further information).

Left: *The Red Lion* at No 1 High Street, pictured in the 1960s, closed in 1980 and was then used as offices before being converted to apartments in 2015.

Below: No 5 High Street was a grocery shop for many decades, trading as Edwards at the time of this 1966 view. It was demolished in the mid-1970s and the site, together with the adjacent property at No 3, was rebuilt in the early 1980s.

Above: High Street, in 1966, looking north, past Barclays Bank (Now converted to apartments, at No 7).

Right:
Emerging from Gunnell's, fruiterer and grocer, at 12/14 High Street dressed in the fashion of the day in 1969.

Left: The Jolly Coopers at 16 High Street with Gunnell's on the southern side of the entrance to the pub car park.

Left: Hampton Motor Works, now rebuilt and used by JP Motors, was originally the first free school for girls in Hampton and was built in 1805.

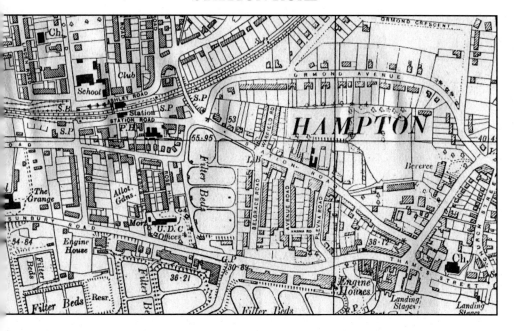

Modern Station Road has a very complex history and has had more names than probably any other road in Hampton. (See also *'The Changing Face of Station Road'*, BOTLHS Paper 93, 2014, for further information).

To start with we'll take a look at the shops and pubs in the road in 1940 from the street directory and then, where the information is available and recorded elsewhere, what had happened as close to the end of the 1960s as possible bearing in mind that 1940 was the last reliable street directory for Hampton.

	1940 – North side	c1969 – North side
70	H A Job, dairy	BV Clarke, menswear c1954 to 1990s
72	Hampton Wallpaper & Paint Stores	A Williams, hairdresser c1953 to c1970

74	F Bonfield, removal contractors	F Bonfield, removals up to 1960s
76	Madame Benn, laundry receiving office	RE Baker, toys 1960s to c1986
78 & 80	W Bonfield, oilman	EW Bonfield & Son, ironmonger to 1980s
82	The Coombe Bakery, bakers	Elizabet Helps, baker c1960 to c1981
88	*Worlds End*	*Worlds End*
92	T J Friston, grocer	Rebuilt L Friston, grocer to early 1960s
94	A Middlemiss (Chemists) Ltd	Rebuilt, Post Office c1950 up to 1993
96	P Tuffin, upholsterer	Rebuilt, GE Lloyd, radio & TV c1950 to c1970
98	Mrs D O Seally, hairdresser	Rebuilt, J Best, florist early 1960s, Hampton Studio, photographers late 1960s
100	Mrs E Adams, confectioner	Rebuilt, Hartley's, greengrocers, from at least c1960-90
	Railway Inn	Demolished, Station Close built on site
	Railway Bell	*Railway Bell*

	1940 – South side	**c1969 – South side**
29	Unoccupied	Minet Cleaners c1954 to c1969
31	A V Barnes, fried fish shop	No details

67-71	London Co-op Society	London Co-op Society to 1979
73	G Yalden, corn dealer	Yaldens, garden supplies to c1970
75	J Hammett & Son, butcher	No details
83	D Brown, greengrocer	D Brown, greengrocer to c1980
85	F W Dore, Newsagent	The Paper Shop to c1995
87	Brumptons, cycle makers	Brumptons, cycle dealers to 1960s
89	G Perrin, draper	No details
91	Unoccupied	No details
93	F H Hadland, grocer	Grocers to 1964 then FJ Edwards, estate agents to c1975
95	Miss G Bond, hairdresser	Miss Bond 1953, Notley & Collins, sports goods 1960s
97	Mrs B A McNaughton, confectioner	Various names as confectioner & tobacconist
99	Unoccupied	Ansell, hairdressers and wool shop in 1960s
101	Unoccupied	Claryl, hairdresser in 1960s
115	J S Friend, fried fish shop	Peter Buchan, fishmonger 1960s to c1986
117	F Warwick, café	Hampton Florists in early 1960s
119	Unoccupied	H A Simester, printer c1953 to at least 1976
121	J Bewsey, butcher	J Bewsey, butcher until c1995
123	C A Falkner, corn dealer	Falkners, corn & garden supplies until 1997

127 *Railway Hotel*	*Railway Hotel*
129 Unoccupied	Keep, toys c1953 to c1969
131a H Maund, tobacconist	**131** The Regent, confectionery & tobacco c1960 to c1995
133 Unoccupied	Various. Cameo, ladies hairdresser from c1967 to 1988
135-7 Unoccupied	T Ware, builders merchants 1950s the Retail tool & building supplies 1960s

Other significant changes in the road during this period included a new turning on land at the rear of 40-44 Station Road, Beaver Close (first recorded in the 1968 Register of Electors); see the 'New Roads' section for further details. A row of four cottages at Nos 60-66 was demolished in 1958 to provide the present parking area at the old police garage beside the former police station. A girl guide hut (now demolished) was erected in the mid-1950s, and officially opened in November 1957, on land behind the present scout hut. It was to be used for training guides and brownies (nine guide companies and eleven brownie packs of the district). Nearby, in 1940, a bomb dropped near the end of Warfield Road. This destroyed the shops at 92, 94, 96, 98 and 100 Station Road as well as *Warfield House* at No 102 and houses in Warfield Road as well. These were all rebuilt after the war although a block of flats built in 1957, Warfield Court, replaced the former *Warfield House*.

On the southern side of Station Road, a row of fourteen terraced houses, numbered 1-27, was demolished in August 1969 and replaced by the flats known as Algar Court in the 1970s. At the other end of the road the Hampton Station Infants' School closed in 1969 when Ripley Road Infants' School opened and the old building was demolished in 1971 and replaced by the block of flats called Rushbury Court at 125 Station Road.

Above: Demolition work on the terraced cottages (1-27 Station Road) in August 1969; Algar Court flats now occupy the site.

Below: The flattened site after the cottages at Nos 1-27 Station Road had been demolished.

Left: Looking up Station Road from outside the former cinema (now Just Curves) towards *The Railway Bell* in the centre far distance in 1964.

Left: The shop of GE Lloyd, TVs and radios, at 96 Station Road, on the corner with Warfield Road in 1969, and is now the Post Office.

Right: Looking towards the Station Road filter beds from the railway bridge. They had been constructed in 1902 and were later filled in and demolished in 1997 for the village green development.

Below: View from the railway bridge towards the station in 1958 with coal merchants on the left on the site now occupied by Kempton Rise flats.

Above: The Station Master's House (now *Station House*) in 1964 with a glimpse of the signal box just left of house.

Below: The Station with the old 1930s concrete footbridge which was replaced with a metal bridge in 2009.

Above: No 123, seen here in 1959, was occupied by Falkner's, seed merchants and garden supplies from 1923 until 1994.

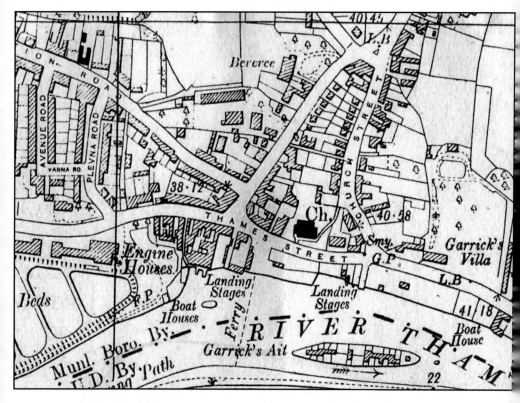

Thames Street, now part of the A308, is another short section of an ancient through road named as it runs beside the Thames through the heart of the historic village of Hampton. It stretches from the western end of Hampton Court Road, at the junction with Church Street, to the junction with Plevna Road where it becomes the Upper Sunbury Road.

For many years Thames Street was Hampton's principal shopping street but the rise of the motor car in this ancient, narrow, twisty road which was dusty in the dry and muddy in the wet led eventually to the building of shops in Station Road as a more viable and pleasant place to shop. Below we'll take a look at the shops and pubs in the road in 1940 from the street directory and then, where the information is available and recorded elsewhere, what had happened as close to the end of the 1960s as possible bearing in mind that 1940 was the last reliable street directory for Hampton.

1940 – North side		c1969 – North side
8	*Bell Hotel*	*Bell Hotel*
10	V G Kenton, confectioner	{ NB The shops at **10-18**
14	Mrs A Robins, refreshment rooms	{ were rebuilt in 1961 as { four flats and a shop (**18**) { occupied by Kenton's
16-18	F Allen, tobacconist	{ sweet shop up to c1995.
24	Mrs A Baynham, dining rooms	No details
28	B Haigelden, tobacconist	No details
34	C A Smallbone Ltd, grocers	C A Smallbone into 1960s then Unwins Ltd, wine shop by 1969
36	E G Newman, greengrocer	E G Newman in 1953, unknown thereafter

1940 – South side		c1969 – South side
3	Mrs D K Haslam, tea rooms	Hampton Tea Gardens in 1953, later offices
5-9	H Lock, boat builder	Demolished in 1946-47
17	A Shepherd, cycle dealer	No details
19	Smith's (Hampton) Ltd, soap works	Soap works closed c1940, became derelict, flats built on site in 1997

21	H Symons, stationer & Post Office	Yorkshire Café 1953, antiques 1959, later converted to house
23	Payne & Williams, butcher	J R Ott Ltd 1953, Foreman & Sons, precision engineers in 1969
25	Miss W M Smith, milliner	No details

NB *The Bell Hotel* still trades today but all the shops listed above are now converted to, or rebuilt as, domestic accommodation.

Significant changes in the road, during this period, included the demolition of two groups of cottages. The shops at 10-18, already alluded to, were rebuilt in 1961 as a block of four flats and a shop. The shop remained until 1995 but has itself now been converted to a flat. At the other end of Thames Street some picturesque old cottages at 44-52, next to the former fire station, were rebuilt as a terrace of houses, set further back from the road, in 1959. The fire station closed after the war but the property, with its distinctive red-painted arched doors, remains in use as commercial premises.

On the south side of Thames Street, as mentioned above, the soap works closed c1940. The premises, and other properties on that side of the road, became rundown and in some cases derelict after a 'road on stilts' was proposed in 1958. This was to run along the riverside and through these properties to 'bypass' Thames Street. The uncertainty from this planning blight was not resolved until the local section of the M25 was built in the early 1980s. Further along, a new turning off Thames Street, Thames Close, was built for some employees at the waterworks and first recorded on the Register of Electors in 1952 (see the section on 'New Roads' for further information).

Above: St Mary's Church, the Vicarage and the old *Feathers Inn* (2-6 Thames Street) in 1966.
Below: View towards *The Red Lion* (centre) from opposite *The Bell* (extreme right) in c1950.

THAMES ST HAMPTON 7.

THAMES STREET, HAMPTON.   HN 18

Above: Looking east towards *The Bell* and St Mary's Church at the junction of Thames Street and High Street in c1950
Below: Thames Street looking west from the side of *The Red Lion* towards the old fire station in the distance in 1966.

Above: The old candle and soap factory (left) and old post office and former butchers shop (centre) with the old fire station (right) in c1963.
Below: Thames Street looking east towards St Mary's Church in c1950.

Above: The site of *Jessamine House*, pictured just before demolition in 1957, is now used by Kingsbury's for displaying cars.

Below: A 1958 plan to build a "road on stilts" along the riverside to "bypass Thames Street" caused a public outcry as it would have ruined the riverside and the proposal was eventually dropped.

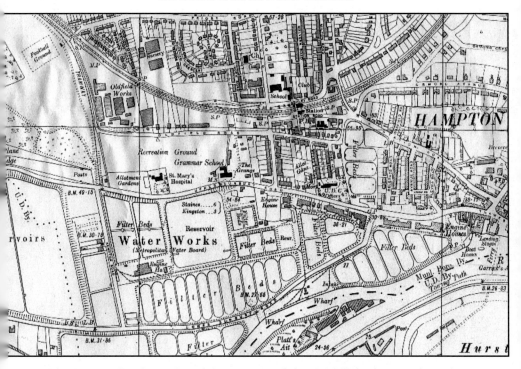

The Upper Sunbury Road (now part of the A308) is the continuation of Thames Street, at its western end near the junction with Plevna Road, running towards Sunbury. In the 1940s, 1950s and 1960s the road was, and still is, dominated by the waterworks that had been constructed from the mid-1850s onwards.

In a road with few houses there was a small amount of building in this period. A new house, *Hampton House* was constructed in the rear garden of *Berkeley House*. Next to *Berkeley House* stood *The Grange* which was taken over by the adjacent Hampton Grammar School and in 1919 plans were submitted for the conversion of the house to be an annexe to the school. The grammar school moved out of its premises (built 1879) into new buildings in Hanworth Road in 1939 at just about the start of WW2. The old premises remained in a variety of uses, mainly in connection with further education, including being part of Twickenham College of Technology, until

1972. The buildings are now demolished and have been replaced by housing.

The next building along from the grammar school was St Mary's Cottage Hospital. The hospital had opened in 1913 as a result of a donation of land, building costs and money from T Foster Knowles, a wealthy resident, who lived at *Riverdale*, No 1 Thames Street. In 1943 T Foster Knowles resigned as Chairman and Trustee and died in 1945. St Mary's Hospital was maintained on a voluntary basis until the inception of the NHS in 1948 when it was taken over by the Ministry of Health.

Many improvements were made to the hospital in the 1960s and the hospital celebrated its Diamond Jubilee in 1973. In 1974 the Health Service was re-organised and St Mary's was transferred to a different Health Authority. It was all down-hill from then on. The details of all these proposals, cuts and changes is a separate subject in itself but suffice it to say, and as is the way with these things, that despite immense community fund raising and cuts and indeed a very large expenditure by the Hampton Fuel Allotment Trust the hospital was eventually closed on 31 March 1994. The buildings survived and they were used in connection with mental health facilities and the premises were renamed St Mary's Lodge. In due course this new usage also ceased and the buildings were boarded-up and abandoned for some time. Eventually the buildings were demolished in 2007 and a new, private, residential home for the elderly called Hampton Care was built on the site and opened in 2008.

Above: A group photo of staff at the waterworks with the clock tower and other Thames Street buildings in the background in c1950.

Right: Looking east, in 1963, along the Upper Sunbury Road, at the junction with Lower Sunbury Road, towards the large house, *Spring Grove*, centre, (demolished 1981).

Above: Looking west along the Upper Sunbury Road towards the junction with Lower Sunbury Road in 1963.

UXBRIDGE ROAD

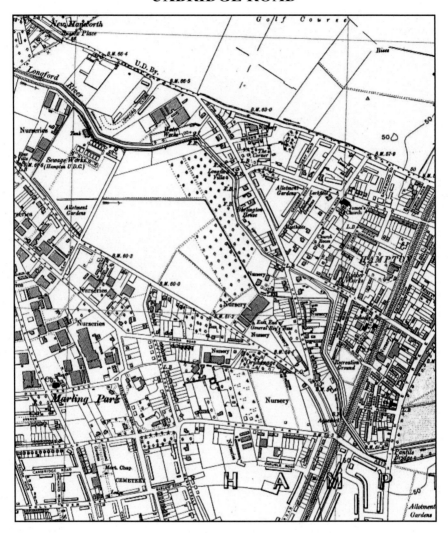

Uxbridge Road is not as old as the other main roads of Hampton. It came about as a result of the enclosure when it was made a 30ft wide road and is shown on the 1826 Enclosure map. Before then, parts of it had existed as tracks, at various times with a variety of names.

In the 1940s, 1950s and 1960s, new turnings were built off Uxbridge Road including Winifred Road (and a turning off it called Graham

Road), Longford Close (built partly just before the war and a whole new section connected to it built after the war), Ringwood Way, Grenville Mews, Arundel Close and The Garth (see the section on 'New Roads' for further information).

At No 195, *Thirlstane House*, plans were submitted for a block of 11 flats in 1964 to replace a house of the same name.

Burlington House at No 177 houses Lady Eleanor Holles (LEH) Junior School and was greatly extended in c1952.

A number of houses were built near the junction with St James's Road during our period as well as the 48 flats at Fairlight at the junction with Windmill Road on the site of a large house of the same name in 1963. Access to the site utilised the then newly built Arundel Close (which first appeared on the 1961 Register of Electors).

Plans were approved for 12 houses in 1939 at 77-87 Uxbridge Road and these had been completed by 1940 when No 87 was damaged by a high explosive bomb. At least two properties (Nos 31 and 33) were rebuilt after the war as a result of war damage. Various other properties were built on other plots during our time period.

Page opposite, above: The junction of Uxbridge Road with High Street (now controlled by traffic lights) in 1963 with the houses of Howard Close behind the hedge.

Page opposite, below: The junction of Uxbridge Road and Broad Lane (to the right), in 1964, near the bridge over the railway before widening, which was completed the following year.

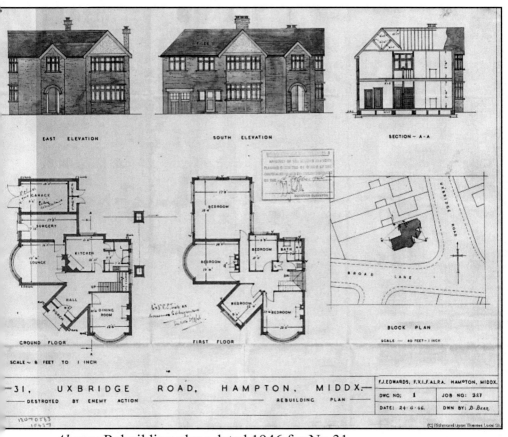

Above: Rebuilding plans dated 1946 for No 31 Uxbridge Road (at the corner of Broad Lane) which was destroyed by enemy action in the war.

Page opposite, above: Looking towards the bridge over the railway in Uxbridge Road where widening works had just started in 1964.

Page opposite, below: The junction of Uxbridge Road and Hanworth Road in 1963.

SOME OTHER ROADS

THE CHANGES THAT occurred, in the 1940s, 1950s and 1960s, in the seven principal roads (Church Street, Hampton Court Road, High Street, Station Road, Thames Street, Upper Sunbury Road and Uxbridge Road) have already been described under 'Main Roads'. The new roads that were built in the same time-period are covered in the 'New Roads' section. We now turn, briefly, to building that took place in other roads that already existed prior to 1940.

It would be invidious, and indeed tedious to the reader, to try to detail every change that occurred in these latter roads and so a brief summary of the types of change that were happening follows.

During WW2 there was little building occurring in Hampton unless it was for the war effort which included some street shelters, underground shelters (eg in Manor Gardens) and air raid warning posts although the latter were often housed in existing buildings or on roof top vantage points. In addition, factories such as that of Hall and Hall in Oldfield Road (which specialised in packing and jointing materials particularly gaskets for engines) continued to expand to enhance production. Bridges, supposedly temporary, were also built to both Tagg's Island and Platt's Eyot, to bring materials on and off the islands more rapidly (to the factory on the former and the boatyard on the latter). The Platt's Eyot bridge still exists and the one to Tagg's Island was replaced by the present structure in 1982.

In the aftermath of the conflict, rebuilding and repair work was carried out to houses that had been destroyed, were so badly damaged that they had to be demolished, or were damaged but capable of repair. There are a couple of sources for this information. The first is the Borough Plans where individual plans are marked as being for rebuilding or reinstatement following war damage. The second source of information is a map of the Borough of Twickenham that has been colour coded to show different categories of damage to individual properties. Having reviewed the plans it is possible to compare the information on them to the map and there was a pleasing similarity between the two (although it is known that not every plan has survived).

Looking at the original map, in particular, it can be seen that there were two areas where a cluster of properties were destroyed. One incident, in 1940, was to some properties in Station Road (including five shops at Nos 92, 94, 96, 98 & 100) and the Station Road end of Warfield Road where the properties were rebuilt after the war. The other major cluster was to houses on either side of Milton Road which were also rebuilt (some as 'aged persons dwellings' in the mid-1950s). Two or more properties together were also destroyed in Dean Road, Falcon Road, Courtlands Avenue, Tudor Avenue, Varna Road and Broad Lane. Individual properties were destroyed in The Avenue (*The White House*), Carlisle Road, Percy Road, Bloxham Crescent, Ormond Crescent, Ormond Drive, Cardinals Walk, Warwick Close and Plevna Road.

New building continued, after the war, on a number of existing roads that had been only partly built up before the war. This was particularly true of the Manor House Estate. Most houses in Ormond Crescent and Ormond Drive were constructed after the war, mainly in the 1950s with a few in the 1940s. A few houses, mainly in the 1940s, were also built in Manor Gardens as well as Cardinals Walk. A couple of sites, near the railway line, were not built on in Ormond Avenue until the early 1960s although, ironically, new housing has already replaced those houses in recent years.

A number of houses were also built in Chestnut Avenue in the 1950s. Longford Close, on which building had commenced just before the war, had a whole new section added after the war. In Percy Road which had had some large houses on very large plots (particularly between Ashley Road and Priory Road on the eastern side) saw these replaced by blocks of flats. At the southern end of

Avenue Road (on the corner site between Avenue Road and Varna Road) a block of flats, Dyer House, was built in the mid-1960s on the site of a former thermostat factory.

In several roads, additional housing was built on former nurseries or plots that had been part of nurseries. This is the case in Buckingham Road, Coombe Road, Nightingale Road (both sides of the northern end of the road), Oak Avenue, Ripley Road (also both sides of the northern end of the road), and South Road.

In Marlborough Road, very large plots at either end of the road were built on. At the southern end a large portion of the plot of *Elm Court* (either side and at the rear), including the former site of the stables, were developed in the early 1960s although the house with its carriage drive front garden still survives. Most of these plots abutted onto, and were designated as being in, Broad Lane. At the other end of the road (on the corner with Old Farm Road) the former site of the large house *Ingoldsby* was developed and the house demolished in the early 1960s.

Oldfield Road had the Oldfield Works of Hall & Hall at its western end and these continued to be extended and altered throughout the war and in the 1950s and 1960s. Closer back to the eastern end but before the junction with Percy Road is reached, on the north side, some additional housing was built as well as a Youth Recreation Centre (a timber-built youth hut).

In Hanworth Road, various extensions and ancillary buildings to the three schools on the northern side, particularly LEH school and Hampton Grammar School (now Hampton School) were built during the period. Housing was also built on the site of *Burleigh House* and on plots that were part of larger plots of other properties.

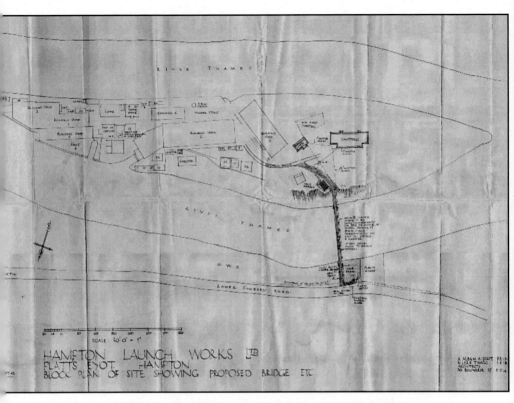

Above: A plan, amended in 1943, for a bridge to Platts Eyot, from
the Lower Sunbury Road, to enable supplies to be transported more
easily to and from the Hampton Launch Works of Thornycroft's.

Above: Map showing properties destroyed and damaged in
Hampton by bombing during the Second World War. Property
marked in red was either totally destroyed or so badly damaged

that demolition was necessary. Property marked in blue was seriously damaged but deemed capable of repair.

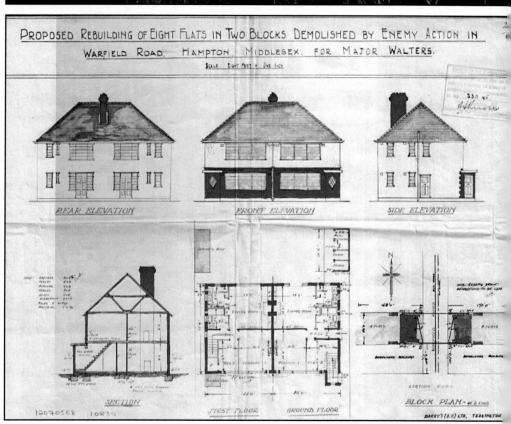

PROPOSED REBUILDING OF EIGHT FLATS IN TWO BLOCKS DEMOLISHED BY ENEMY ACTION IN WARFIELD ROAD, HAMPTON, MIDDLESEX, FOR MAJOR WALTERS.

SCALE EIGHT FEET = ONE INCH

REAR ELEVATION   FRONT ELEVATION   SIDE ELEVATION

SECTION   FIRST FLOOR   GROUND FLOOR   BLOCK PLAN ~ 41 to 1 inch

STATION ROAD

BARRY'S (S.R) LTD, TEDDINGTON.

Above: A block of homes 'for aged persons' built c1956 in Milton Road to replace properties destroyed by bombing in the war.

Page opposite, above: The old wartime bailey bridge (shown here in c1965), from Hampton Court Road to Tagg's Island, was built to assist with the movement of goods and materials to the munitions factory housed on the island during the war.

Page opposite, below: A 1945 plan for the proposed rebuilding of eight flats in two blocks, at the Station Road end of Warfield Road which, along with shops and other properties in Station Road, had been destroyed by a high explosive bomb in 1940.

Right: The Avenue being surfaced for the first time in 1963; previously it had led, mainly, to nurseries and had remained unsurfaced.

Below: Ingoldsby was a large house at the corner of Marlborough Road and Old Farm Road demolished in 1962 shortly after this photo was taken, and replaced by housing.

NEW ROADS

URING THE 1940s, 1950s and 1960s there was much demand for housing but not always the supply. In the immediate aftermath of the war there was a great deal of rebuilding and repair of existing stock to take care of. There was also a shortage of materials and a lack of supply of land as well. Overall, in this period 42 new roads were built in Hampton. By decade, this was split into five in the 1940s, ten in the 1950s and 27 in the 1960s.

The 1940s

The first road to appear in the Electoral Registers after the war was Kingswood Avenue (Map 4, Ref B2) which now runs between Broad Lane and Queenswood Avenue (built later). Much of the land on which the properties were built was formerly wooded and so this may be a factor in the name of the road. Another factor may be that King George VI was on the throne when the road was first named. It is first recorded on the 1945-46 Register of Electors (there being no registers from 1940 up to 1945). However, this is somewhat misleading in the sense that there were only one or two names on the registers in the first ten years and then more in 1955 and a large number by 1956. So, the overwhelming bulk of the properties were not built until the mid-1950s.

The first roads to be built and substantially populated after the war were four roads that were first occupied in 1948. These were Roy Grove (4, B2) and Cannon Close (4, B2), turnings off the Hanworth Road, and Bishops Grove (3, A1) and Rectory Grove (3, A1), turnings off Dean Road. The first two roads take their names from General Roy and his connection with Cannon Field, the land on which they were built. Cannon Field was so called because the barrel of a cannon that is buried upright and projects about three feet into the air in what has become Roy Grove. The cannon marks one end of the original base line used for measurement by triangulation upon which all Ordnance Survey maps were subsequently based. The land at the Hampton end of the base line was Charities Land which was developed by the Council as a housing estate in 1947-48.

The other two roads, Bishops Grove and Rectory Grove, take their ecclesiastical name from the land on which they were built which was part of what was originally known as Rectory Farm. It had come to Hampton Grammar School c1816 as compensation for the loss of the rectorial tithes at the Enclosure. Part of this land was later developed as a Sewage Works which opened in 1899 and closed in 1940 after the new Mogden sewage works came into operation and thus the land became available for development. Three schools (Hampton Grammar School, Rectory School [now Hampton High] and Lady Eleanor Holles) were built on the adjoining land in the late 1930s.

Above: The sewage works, off the Hanworth Road, which had opened in 1899 and closed in 1940 after the new Mogden sewage works came into operation thus freeing up land for development.

The 1950s

The first half on the 1950s saw only one new road (Thames Close (Map 2, Ref B3), in 1952) and it was built by the Metropolitan Water Board (MWB), and not by the Council, as housing for employees (numbered 1-7 Thames Close in a 1953 Directory) on very generously sized plots. Later, in the mid-1990s, the properties were demolished and re-developed as blocks of apartments.

In 1955 Garden Close (3, A2), a turning off Hanworth Road, is first recorded on the Register of Electors. The name presumably recalls the nursery garden that used to occupy this site. This was followed the next year, 1956, by Buckingham Close (3, A2) which is a turning off Buckingham Road, after which it is named. It too was formerly used as a nursery.

House building was now getting up more of a head of steam and five roads first appear in 1957. These were Priory Gardens and Priory Close (both 1, A3), Winifred Road (3, B1) and Graham Road (3, A1) and also Queenswood Avenue (4, B2). In December 1954 Shepherds Ltd of East Molesey submitted plans to build Priory Gardens and a short cul-de-sac, Priory Close, off that road. The 4 ½ acre plot, used as a nursery, was off Priory Road widening considerably behind the rear gardens of houses in Priory Road and reaching down to the railway line to the south. The plot was flanked by the gardens of houses in Broome Road to the west and those in Bloxham Crescent to the east. The plans were amended in March 1955 and the roads were both first listed on the 1957 Register of Electors. Winifred Road is a turning off a service road off Uxbridge Road and Graham Road is a small turning off Winifred Road. They are both named after Winifred Graham who was an author of 88 books, who lived in the house *St Albans* in Hampton Court Road, which was demolished in 1972. She died in 1950 and the two roads commemorate her name and were built on the site of a former nursery. Queenswood Avenue, a turning off Broad Lane adjoining Kingswood Avenue, was built on land on which was formerly allotment gardens. The 1957 Register records only the block of flats known as Faraday House. By 1958 all four blocks (Faraday, Wren, Lytton and Wolsey) are listed.

Douai Grove (2, B3) is a turning off High Street that is first recorded on the 1958 Register of Electors (for which the qualifying date was October 1957) with one house. The road itself had certainly been opened earlier as a plaque, on the rear wall of *Grove House* in High Street which backs onto Douai Grove, records it as opened on 22 March 1956. It is named after *Douai House* which was demolished in order to provide access to the land beside, and at the back of, *Grove House*. The planning application to convert *Grove House* to offices and to build Douai Grove was the subject of a public inquiry in 1956. The controversial plans, which were the prime reason for the founding of the then Hampton Residents Association (now Hampton Society), were approved by the Minister and Douai Grove was built. Later plans, in 1966, to demolish *Grove House* and build 24 houses on the site were rejected and *Grove House* remained as offices until recent years when it was converted back to a single-family residence.

Finally, in the 1950s, Cotswold Road (4, B2) which is a turning off Buckingham Road, is first recorded in the 1959 Register of Electors. It was built on the very substantial plot of a very large house called *Brompton House*.

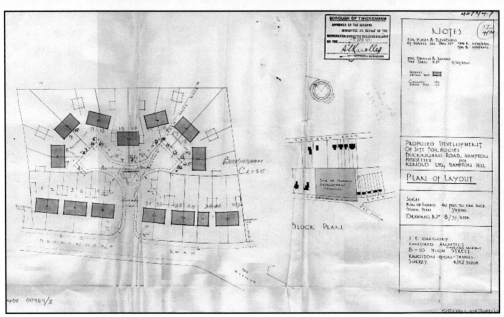

Above: Plans for Buckingham Close, off Buckingham Road, built on the site of a former nursery; the road first appeared in the 1956 Register of Electors.

Below: Priory Gardens and Priory Close, off Priory Road, were also built on the site of a nursery and first appeared in 1957.

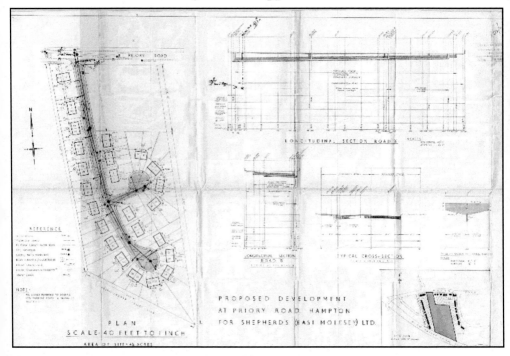

WINIFRED GRAHAM
MRS. THEODORE CORY

Recent Photograph

Left: Winifred Graham, after whom both Winifred and Graham Roads are named, was an author who lived in the house called *St Albans* in Hampton Court Road and died in 1950. The roads first appeared in 1957.

Below: The blocks of flats in Queenswood Avenue, off Broad Lane, under construction in 1957.

Above: Douai House, right, gave its name to Douai Grove, off High Street that first appears in the 1958 Register of Electors. The cottages on the left of the picture still survive.

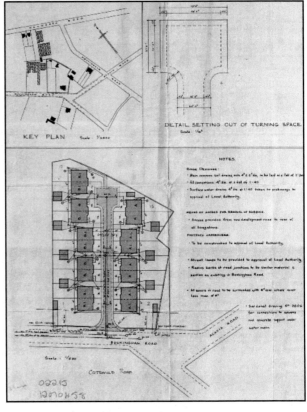

Right: Plans for Cotswold Road, which first appears in 1959, built on the site of a large house called *Brampton House.*

The 1960s

The pace of house building was picking up by the 1960s, particularly with the sale of land formerly used for nurseries. These businesses were facing increasing competition from other countries, particularly those with much lower labour costs which the increasing use of air freight made possible. This factor together with increasing demand for housing meant that many of these sites became available to build on. In all, twenty seven new roads are first recorded on the Electoral Registers during this decade. When looking at these changes it becomes apparent that it was obviously fashionable to call many of these development 'Closes' as almost two thirds of them have the word 'Close' in their name.

In 1961 Markhole Close (Map 1, Ref A3), a turning off Priory Road, is first recorded. The road is built on the land and site of a large house, *Hatherop House,* which gave its name to nearby Hatherop Road formally called Markhole Lane. The name Markhole refers to the hollow on the "mark" or boundary stone with Hanworth; a description which exactly fitted the land west of the lane against Kempton Park. Arundel Close (4, B2), a turning off Uxbridge Road, is also first mentioned in 1961. Here, one half of a pair of semi-detached cottages on the Uxbridge Road was demolished to make the entrance roadway to Arundel Close to access a site formerly used as nursery land.

1962 saw four new roads: Cleves Way, Marlingdene Close, Hollybank Close and Ringwood Way. Cleves Way (1, A3) is a turning off Priory Road built on the site of a former nursery. It is believed that the road is named after Anne of Cleves (1515-1557), fourth wife of Henry VIII. Marlingdene Close (1, A2), a turning off Broad Lane, and some new houses on Broad Lane utilised the plots of two very large houses on Broad Lane. The new close enabled access to land behind the two houses that were demolished. It has a name that derives from the Marling family who were owners of Marling Park (formerly known as Tangley Park and before that as Chalk Farm). Marling Park refers to the large area of land, north of

Broad Lane, between Oak Avenue and Uxbridge Road. The Marling family acquired this estate in the 1890s and gradually tried to develop it, although development was very slow and large amounts of the undeveloped land were used as nurseries. Hollybank Close (3, A2) is a turning off Hanworth Road. The name relates to the florist business and related cottage called Holly Bank that formerly occupied this site. Ringwood Way (4, B1) is a turning off a service road off Uxbridge Road. The land was formerly occupied by a nursery called Ringwood Nursery.

In 1963 Bluefield Close (4, B2), a turning off Buckingham Road, is first recorded. It was built on the site of a former nursery.

1964 had four new roads recorded: Dukes Close, Haslemere Close, Regency Close and Kings Paddock. The name of Dukes Close (3, A1), a turning off Buckingham Road, is probably related to the fact that the close is a turning off Buckingham Road. It is built on the sites of two very large houses, *Ewood* and 190 Buckingham Road. Haslemere Close (3, A2) is another turning off Buckingham Road that occupies the site of a former nursery. Regency Close (3, A1) is a turning off Hanworth Road that utilised the site of a very large house and garden. In the early 1960s work started on what was effectively an extension to Park Close and became Kings Paddock (2, B3), a group of blocks of flats with an outlet via Park Close onto High Street. The Kings Paddock flats first appeared on the 1964 Register of Electors. Nowadays, Park Close is separately listed with the Kings Paddock flats bracketed under it in the register. During WW2 and subsequently, the land now occupied by the Kings Paddock flats was used as a timber yard with large quantities of wood stored there.

In 1965 there were two new roads: Garside Close and The Garth. Garside Close (2, B2) is a turning off Broad Lane named after Bernard Garside (1898-1963), a very prominent Hampton local historian. He was a Yorkshireman who came to Hampton Grammar School in 1924 at the age of 26. He did a prodigious amount of research on the history of Hampton, particularly relating to the

16th and 17th centuries and published ten books on the subject and a further two on the history of the School. In 1962 he founded the Hampton Research Group, a branch of the then newly-formed Borough of Twickenham Local History Society. He died at one of the Hampton Research Group meetings in 1963 at the age of 64. The following year a new road, Garside Close, was named in his memory which first appears on the 1965 Register of Electors. It was built on the former Manor Farm Nursery which was part of the former Manor House Estate. The Garth (4, B2) is a turning off the Uxbridge Road, although somewhat perversely the Register of Electors records The Garth under Uxbridge Road and not as a separate road. The land was previously Gill's Nursery.

1966 was the first year in which Station Close (2, B3) appears. It is a turning off Station Road and is built on land formerly occupied by *The Railway Inn* in Station Road. The beer house was built around the time the railway came to Hampton in 1864 (it is mentioned in an 1868 Directory) and was demolished c1960.

In 1967 four new roads first appear: Albury Close, Holles Close, Jillian Close and Templar Place. Albury Close (4, B2) is a turning off Broad Lane and in 1888 Mr J F Ellis who had been an assistant master at the grammar school, started a boy's preparatory school in Broad Lane, Pembroke House School. The school flourished for more than 70 years and was closed in 1966 to allow demolition and the building of new houses in Broad Lane and the new road Albury Close. Holles Close (4, B2) is a turning off Hanworth Road, opposite the Lady Eleanor Holles School. The road takes its name from the School that had originally been established in 1711 in Cripplegate as a result of a bequest by Lady Holles in 1708, and later moved to Hackney. In 1936-37 it moved to Teddington where it initially occupied the premises of a private school called Summerleigh at 54 Hampton Road. In September 1937 the School moved to the present site in Hanworth Road. The new road was built on the site of a large house and garden. Jillian Close (2, B3) is a turning off Chestnut Avenue built on the site of a very large house and garden called *The Bungalow*. Templar Place (2, B2) is a turning

94

off Tudor Avenue and it is believed that the name of the road is derived from the Knights Templar through which there is a connection to Hampton (as owners of the estate that subsequently became Hampton Court Palace and the surrounding parklands). The road was built on land behind some of the properties in Tudor Avenue.

There were a further four new roads in 1968: Beaver Close, Hawthorn Close, Newfield Close and Wensleydale Gardens. Beaver Close (2, B3) is a turning off Station Road and takes its name from the adjacent football grounds called Beveree and home to Hampton and Richmond Borough F C – "The Beavers". In turn this nick-name is presumably derived from "Beveree" the name of the house (in High Street now occupied by Twickenham Preparatory School) to which the land now used by the football club was once attached. The properties were built on part of the former rear gardens of the cottages at 40-44 Station Road. Hawthorn Close (3, A2) is a turning off Buckingham Road and the name is presumably a reference to the tree of the same name. It is built on the site of a former nursery. Newfield Close (1, A3) is a turning off Percy Road. Originally this land was part of the Oldfield, although the land called Newfield was not too far distant. The site was previously used as Station Nursery. Wensleydale Gardens (2, B3) is a turning off Wensleydale Road. The name Wensleydale comes from a former owner of the Manor House Estate on whose land Wensleydale Gardens and other surrounding roads were later built. In 1845 the owner of the estate died and left the Manor House Estate (sometimes known as the Manor Park Estate) to George James Howard who was then about two years old. His trustee was Baron Parke who later became Lord Wensleydale. The land was previously used as a nursery.

Three new roads appeared in 1969: Beard's Hill Close, Grenville Mews and Johnsons Drive. Beard's Hill Close (2, B3) is a turning off Beard's Hill named after John Beard, the great tenor for whom Handel composed parts in his oratorios. John Beard came to Hampton in about 1768, when deafness was ending his singing career, and lived at the house later known as *Rosehill*. (The building had become the Hampton Council Offices and Library in 1902 and is still the Hampton Library.) In 1903 the Council built 56 "workmen's dwellings" on the former front garden of *Rosehill* in two parallel roads called Rosehill and Beard's Hill. The land on which the new close was built was formerly allotment gardens. Grenville Mews (4, B2) is a turning off Uxbridge Road. The land was formerly associated with St Mary's College (Girls). In the late 1930s Lady Eleanor Holles (LEH) School took over much of the site and in the late 1960s Grenville Mews was built on some of the site. Johnsons Drive (2, B3) is a turning off Church Street. It is built on part of the Garrick's Villa estate. The owner of Garrick's Villa first attempted to obtain approval to build houses on the estate in 1946 and despite repeated new plans, the latest in 1964, they were all refused. A further plan, allowing a more open view of The Orangery, was submitted in 1966 and Hampton Residents Association offered no objection; before long the building of houses forming Johnsons Drive had started.

Two further roads first appeared on the 1970 Register of Electors. However, as the qualifying date was 10 October 1969 then, clearly, they already had at least some residents before the end of the decade. These roads were Hogarth Way and Scotts Drive. Hogarth Way (2, B3) is a turning off Hampton Court Road and, like nearby Johnsons Drive (detailed above), was built on part of the Garrick's Villa estate as part of the same planning applications. Scotts Drive (2, B2) forms an extension to Carlisle Road which is a turning off Gloucester Road. The land was formerly used as a nursery.

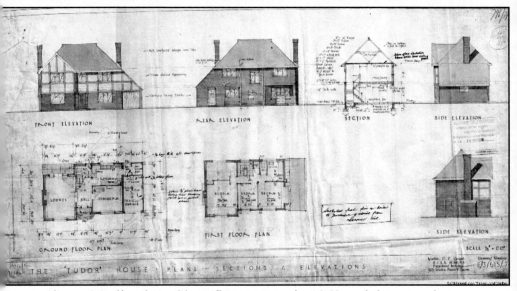

Above: Marlingdene Close first appears in 1962 and the name is a reference to the Marling family who tried to develop much of the land in the 1890s in the area then known as Marling Park.

Below: Bluefield Close, off Buckingham Road, first appears in 1963 and was built on the site of a former nursery.

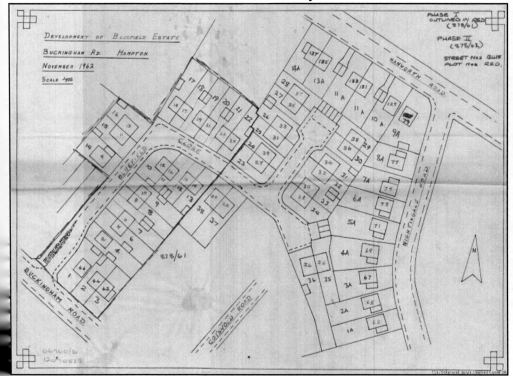

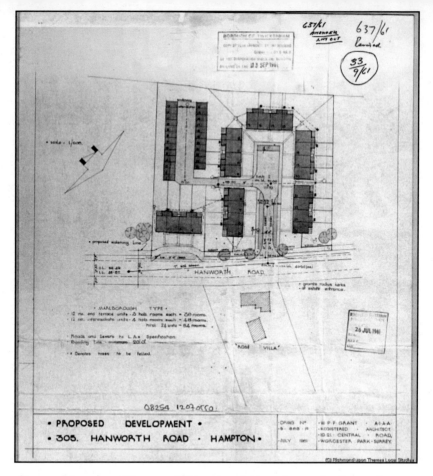

Above: Regency Close, off Hanworth Road, was built on the site of a very large house and garden and first appears in 1964.

Page opposite, above: Kings Paddock is effectively an extension to Park Close, off High Street, and the blocks of flats first appear in 1964.

Page opposite, below: Bernard Garside (1898-1963) was a prolific Hampton local historian who wrote a series of ten books on Hampton in the sixteenth and seventeenth centuries (published between 1937 and 1958) as well as two histories of Hampton Grammar School. Garside Close, off Broad Lane, first appeared in 1965 and is named after him.

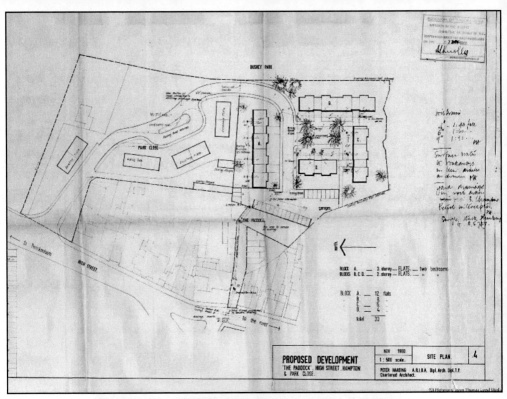

PROPOSED DEVELOPMENT
'THE PADDOCK', HIGH STREET, HAMPTON
& PARK CLOSE.

NOV. 1960.
1 : 500 scale.

SITE PLAN.

4

PETER HARDING A.R.I.B.A. Dipl.Arch. Dist.T.P.
Chartered Architect.

BLOCK A. — 3 storey — FLATS — two bedrooms
BLOCKS B.C.D. — 2 storey — FLATS. — "

BLOCK A. — 12 flats
B. — 8
C. — 6
D. — 4
total 30

99

Above: Pembroke House School occupied a large property in Broad Lane and after its closure and demolition in 1966 it provided the site for additional housing in Broad Lane and a new road, Albury Close. *Below:* Wensleydale Gardens, off Wensleydale Road, was built on the site of a former nursery and first appeared in 1968.

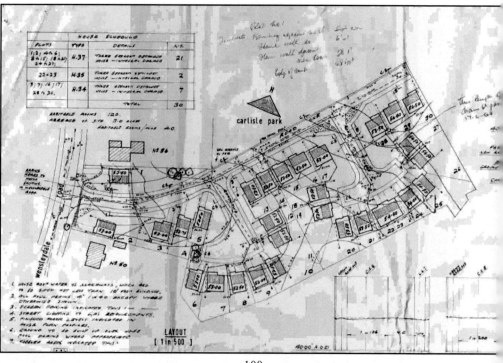

Right:
Johnsons Drive, off Church Street, is built on part of the Garrick's Villa estate and first appeared in 1969. The sign indicates the houses were priced at £8700 - £9400.

Right: Hogarth Way, off Hampton Court Road, is also built on part of the Garrick's Villa estate and is first recorded in the 1970 Register of Electors for which the qualifying date was in October 1969. The image here was taken in April 1971.

PEOPLE AT WORK – BUSINESSES AND SHOPS

IN THE PERIOD 1940s, 1950s and 1960s, Hampton lost three pubs: *The Kings Arms* at 141 Uxbridge Road, *The Jolly Gardeners* at 8 High Street and *The Railway Inn* at 108 Station Road.

The Kings Arms was built, probably in the 1860s, on the west side of the Uxbridge Road near the junction with Windmill Road. The landlord, Thomas King, went bankrupt in 1871. It closed in 1954 and was converted initially into use as a newsagents and greengrocers shop. The property since extended and known as Kings House and Kings Court has been used for office purposes and for domestic accommodation.

The Jolly Gardeners formerly occupied the premises now known as 8 and 8A High Street. It is not known when *The Jolly Gardeners* came into existence. It occupied what is an ancient, probably 17ᵗʰ century, property possibly set up as a beer house after 1830 when the Beer House Act was passed. The landlord was Thomas Bridgeman in 1890 when the Jolly Gardeners was sold to Ashby's (the brewers) of Staines for £1500. When Thomas Bridgeman died in 1910 he was recorded as being a Crimean War veteran. *The Jolly Gardeners* was taken over by Charles Peter Heath in 1936 and the pub closed in 1955. The premises were subsequently used as C.P. Heath, the boat builder, and are still partly occupied by the Heath family.

Contrary to what might be thought, the beer house that became *The Railway Inn* in Station Road was in existence prior to the coming of the railway in 1864. We know this from a plan in the Manor Court books in 1862 that shows "The Two Elms" beer house, as the property was then called. The coming of the railway did, however, lead to a change in name. Plans for alterations were approved in

1888 and they show a large new building to be joined onto the earlier one. The completed layout had about three times the floor area of the original building. *The Railway Inn*, was popularly known as "Bob Barrett's" after Robert Barrett, the landlord since 1922, and was demolished c1960. The cul-de-sac Station Close was then built on the site.

Other pubs continued to trade throughout our time period and are still in business today. These are *The Bell* at 8 Thames Street (rebuilt in 1893 after a fire in 1892), *The Jolly Coopers* at 16 High Street (originally called *The Glass and Bottle*), *The Worlds End* at 88 Station Road (rebuilt in 1914), *The Railway Bell* in Station Road (originally built as one of the cottages in the Yew Tree Cottages block) and *The Royal Oak* in Oak Avenue (built as the Royal Oak Stores and which gained a licence in 1914).

A number of other pubs were trading in the 1940s, 1950s and 1960s but have since closed. These were *The Red Lion* at 1 High Street, closed in 1980 and converted to apartments in 2015, *The White Hart* at 70 High Street which was converted to White Hart House in 2005 as well as *The Dukes Head* at 122 High Street which was converted to domestic accommodation in 2015. There was also *The Railway* at 127 Station Road which was converted to flats called Junction Court in 2011 and *The Jolly Gardeners* at 94 Uxbridge Road, closed in 2000, and converted to domestic accommodation.

The oldest business in Hampton is Hampton Ferry which has run continuously for 500 years and was already in existence in 1519. The business was substantially affected by the closure of the Hurst Park racecourse in 1962 (see 'People at Play – Recreation and Celebration' section for further information on the ferry) but continues running to this day.

During the war bridges were built to both Platt's Eyot (the plans being approved in 1943) and Tagg's Island, to bring materials on and off the islands more rapidly. Initially the plans included a pipe for the water main to be laid temporarily on the bed of the river across to Platt's Eyot and this was later to be fixed permanently to the side of the bridge when built. The island was home to Thornycroft's and had a number of boat building shops and associated workshops. Between the wars the yard had built the finest civilian craft to the highest standards as well as naval vessels and numbers of both types of craft were exported to many countries as well as being built for use in this country. During wartime all boat building for civilian purposes had to cease and Thornycroft's built MTBs (Motor Torpedo Boats) and other naval craft throughout WW2 and beyond. In the 1960s Thornycroft's was taken over by Vospers and boat building, apart from some repair work, ceased on the island.

On Tagg's Island there had been an hotel and entertainment complex, originally called the Karsino, which opened in 1913. It later had various name changes and had become the Casino Hotel by the time the island was acquired by William Hurlock of AC Cars Ltd in 1940. The covered tennis court and the skating rink were then adapted to the making of munitions of various kinds and after the war these facilities were turned to making 'invalid cars' for the victims of the war. A 'temporary' Bailey bridge first connected the island to the riverside during WW2. In November 1965 the closure of the bridge was ordered as the Council considered it unsafe and the following month it collapsed into the river. It was repaired and re-opened in March 1966 and it lasted until a new bridge was constructed in the early 1980s.

During our time period the factory of Hall and Hall in Oldfield Road (which specialised in packing and jointing materials particularly gaskets for engines) continued to expand to enhance production and was a major employer. In 1937 a precision tool company, Gay Brothers, had been established next door and this too later expanded. In c1932 *Castle House* in High Street had been converted into offices and the grounds into a sawmill and timber yard by the Hampton Timber Company. They sold the property to Messrs Lovell & Sons Ltd in 1957 and the house was later demolished in c1960 and an industrial works built on the site which has since been rebuilt/converted to become Castle Business Village. The waterworks, which came to Hampton in the mid-1850s, continued to be major employers although there was pressure to cut numbers employed through mechanisation and enhanced processes.

House rebuilding and repair after all the damage caused by the war, particularly in the late 1940s and into the early 1950s, as well as the building of new houses, especially in the later 1950s and 1960s, was conducted on a large scale and many people were employed in this way. The nurseries, of which there were still 45 in business in 1939, were still large employers. During the conflict they were not allowed to grow their usual crops of flowers and so salad crops, in particular, were grown instead. After the war, competition from overseas increased, eg from Holland and, with the growth of airfreight, from countries much further afield with lower labour costs. Many of the nurseries were involved in significant innovation but despite this overseas competition was unremitting. The nurseries struggled on into the 1960s and a few into the 1970s but most had become unprofitable, and many derelict, by around 1970. The derelict sites were eventually built on, as part of the Nurserylands housing development in c1980 onwards.

In addition to those mentioned above there were other significant businesses, some long-running, eg Kingsbury's garage in Station Road, and of course there were a variety of shops and small enterprises. Many of the shops are more fully described in the 'Main Roads' section.

Mention should also be made of shops in other roads (not in the 'Main Roads' section) particularly the cluster of shops close to the station in Ashley Road, Milton Road, Station Approach and Wensleydale Road and the much smaller separate cluster, slightly further from the station, in Priory Road. Space does not permit detailing all these, however a few long-lasting ones can be mentioned.

In Ashley Road, Pearkes Stores Ltd, a grocers, was a long-running business as were a few of the businesses at or near the station itself, including the kiosk of WH Smith, Hughes & Tickner, estate agents, and Harold Newton, builders' merchants.

In Milton Road most shops stayed in the same business throughout our time period. No 70 was Charles Kent, hairdresser, from 1940 until the 1960s and Budd, radio & electrical from then right up to the mid-1990s. No 72 was a newsagents throughout and remains so to this day and No 74 was a butchers, firstly as F & G Toms and then as RE Grimes. No 76 was Scott, domestic stores, from 1940 into the 1960s and No 80 was AE Keeping, grocers from 1940 until the 1960s.

The Station Approach shops, on the north side – Nos 1, 2 & 3 – have all stayed in the same business since they were built in 1928: as an off-licence, bakers and a chemist. On the south side Thompsons, tobacconist and confectioner, at No 6 was the same throughout as was Iris Mae, ladies and children's outfitters, at No 8.

Wensleydale Road also had a number of shops that were in business throughout all or most of our time period including Lloyds Bank, Hampton Electrical Supplies, a grocers, Adams, confectioners, and F J Bonfield, photographic supplies.

Priory Road was also home to several long-running shops including Westminster Wine Co at No 21 (on the corner with Tudor Road) and No 23 Grimditch, a butchers (on the corner with Milton Road). At No 33 was the Post Office throughout the 20th century until it closed in 2004, No 37 was J Prewett & Sons, dairymen from 1940 until the 1960s and No 39 was G Cornish & Son, bakers and confectioners for the whole time. On the other side of the road, No 28B was a chemists throughout and remains as such today. Further down the road Watchorn, a butcher, was in business throughout as was A W Hughes (later Wallingtons), fried fish shop at No 104.

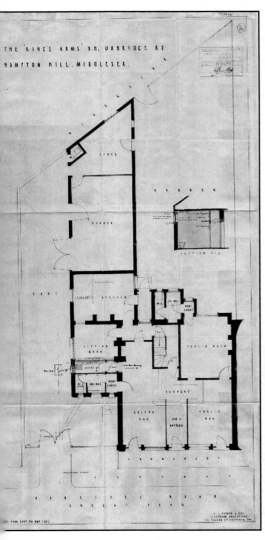

THE KINGS ARMS P.H. UXBRIDGE RD
HAMPTON HILL. MIDDLESEX.

Left: A floor plan showing the bar layout for *The Kings Arms* at 141 Uxbridge Road which closed in 1954.

Right: The Jolly Gardeners at 8 High Street which closed in 1955 and is now used as housing (8 and 8a High Street).

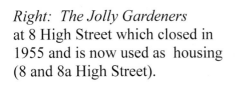

Above: The Railway Inn at 108 Station Road was demolished c1960 and is now occupied by the housing in Station Close.

Left: The Bell at 8 Thames Street in c1950 was rebuilt in 1893 after a fire at the old premises in 1892.

Right: The Jolly Coopers at 16 High Street, in c1973, is the longest-running Hampton pub still in its original premises.

Below: The Worlds End which was rebuilt in 1914 on the site of earlier premises is pictured in c1969.

Page opposite, above: The Railway Bell, in Station Road, pictured in 1966, was originally part of the Yew Tree Cottages terrace.

Page opposite, below: The Royal Oak in Oak Avenue in 1950 showing a ceremony to commemorate two men who had been killed in 1940 just outside the pub by a high explosive bomb.

Below: The Red Lion at 1 High Street shown in c1950 was closed in 1980, then used as offices and converted to apartments in 2015.

Above: The Railway Hotel, in 1953, was later converted into flats called Junction Court in 2011.

Page opposite, above: The White Hart at 70 High Street was converted to apartments in 2005 and is now known as White Hart House.

Page opposite, below: The Dukes Head at 122 High Street was converted to domestic accommodation in 2015 and is pictured here in c1974.

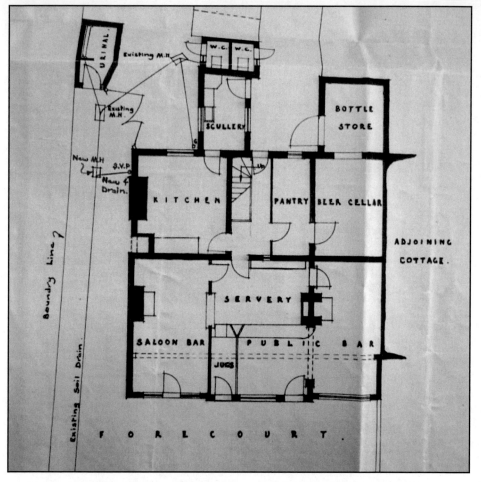

Above: A floor plan showing the bar layout of *The Jolly Gardeners* at 94 Uxbridge Road which closed in 2000 and was converted to domestic accommodation.

Page opposite, above: ML (Motor Launch) 1133 was built at Platts Eyot by Thornycroft's and completed on 27 June 1942. It was 72 ft long and 15 ft 6 ins wide (22 m x 4.7 m).

Page opposite, below: HMS Puttenham was an inshore minesweeper for the Royal Navy, built at Thornycroft's, launched on 25 June 1956. It was of all-wood construction, 107 ft 6 in (32.8 m) in length with a beam of 22 ft (6.7 m) and a draught of 5 ft 9 in (1.8 m).

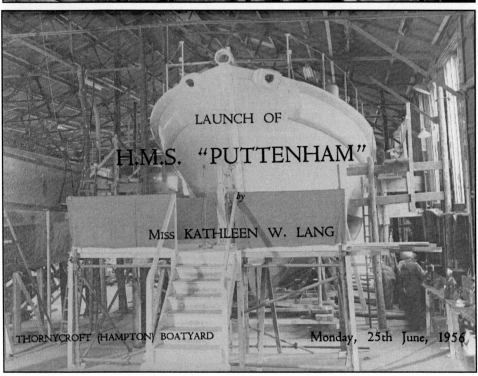

LAUNCH OF

H.M.S. "PUTTENHAM"

by

Miss KATHLEEN W. LANG

THORNYCROFT (HAMPTON) BOATYARD   Monday, 25th June, 1956.

The Casino Hotel, Taggs Island, Hampton Court.

Above: The Casino Hotel, originally built as the Karsino by Fred Karno, was a hotel and entertainment complex on Tagg's Island where some of the facilities were turned over for use as a munitions factory during the war.

Page opposite, above: The old bailey bridge to Tagg's Island, built during the war, collapsed in December 1965 and was then reinstated and finally replaced in the early 1980s.

Page opposite, below: A postcard illustrating the premises of the Hampton Timber Co Ltd in c1950 in High Street. Today the site is occupied by Castle Business Village.

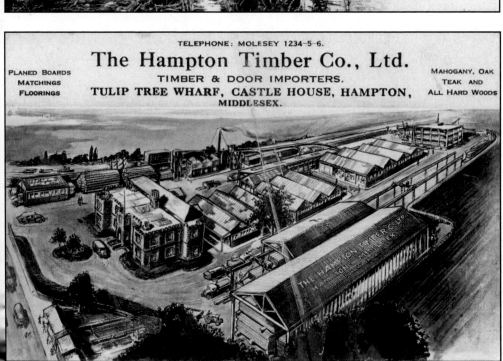

Above: Fred Mason, manager of K E Page's nursery, Oak Avenue, with a group of land girls working at the site in the 1940s.

Page opposite, above: Red and white carnations in one of the glasshouses at the nursery of K E Page in 1958.

Page opposite, below: Deep snow during the exceptionally cold winter of 1962-63 at the nursery of K E Page almost prevented the vital coal deliveries to power the boilers to heat the pipes in the glasshouses.

Above: Outside potting of chrysanthemums at the nursery of K E Page in 1964. The scale of this exercise can be judged by the number of pots already growing.

Below: Unloading boxes of flowers outside the shops at Ashley Road in 1969.

Above: Queues outside the very long established butcher's shop of R E Grimes in Milton road in 1969.

Below: A delivery in 1969 at the wine shop of Ellis's at No 1 Station Approach which has been an off-licence continuously since the shop was built in 1928.

Left: The shops in Wensleydale Road, shown here in 1966, then included both Barclays and Lloyds Bank. Both are now closed, Lloyds only shut in 2019.

Below: A queue outside Priory Road Post Office in 1969 along with a fine array of prams, pushchairs, bikes and trikes.

People at Play - Recreation and Celebration

Celebrations and Processions

THE EVENTS BELOW, all celebrated in Hampton, were all connected with national events.

The end of the Second World War was declared, in Europe, on 8 May 1945 (VE Day) although victory over Japan was not declared until 15 August (VJ Day). This was recorded in the school log book at Hampton Junior School as: *"May 8, 9 School was closed on these two days, which were public holidays in celebration of Victory in the European War. The Union Jack was hoisted on the school building"*. There was much celebration after all the years of loss, misery and deprivation and street parties and parades were held all over the country. A more formal, official, celebration was held the following year called the London Victory Celebrations of 1946. It was described as *"British Commonwealth, Empire and Allied victory celebrations held after the defeat of Nazi Germany and Japan in World War II."* The celebrations took place in London on 8 June 1946, and consisted mainly of a military parade through the city and a night time fireworks display. Hampton, part of the Borough of Twickenham, held its own celebrations as did the rest of the borough and other places throughout the country.

On Saturday 8 June in Hampton there was open-air dancing in Carlisle Park from 8pm to 11pm. It was also advertised that the main thoroughfares in the Borough would have street decorations and that there would be floodlighting of churches, buildings and gardens. In Bushy Park, near the Lion Gates, there were races for children and then adults as well as a baby show, side shows and community singing followed by dancing at 7.30pm. Sunday 9 June saw a

'Victory Drumhead Service' in Carlisle Park at 3pm (a drumhead service being a religious service attended by members of the military). Children's events were held on 10 June, also in Carlisle Park, starting with a grand youth procession at 2pm with the mayor taking the salute. This was followed by children's sports, with prizes, from 3pm to 5.30pm and a children's variety concert from 6pm to 8pm. There was dancing from 8pm to 10pm as well as band performances, numerous side shows and a firework display and the grounds were floodlit. For the children, especially, it must have been a day to remember.

The Festival of Britain of 1951, held a few years after the war, was the key cultural event of the period. The original plan was to celebrate the centenary of the Great Exhibition of 1851. However, it was not to be another World Fair, and instead the 1951 Festival focused entirely on Britain and its achievements. The goal of the Festival was to give the people a feeling of successful recovery from the war's devastation as well as promoting British science, technology, industrial design, architecture and the arts. Nationwide, *"a programme of events was skilfully planned with the aim of embracing modernist influences on British culture whilst also clinging nostalgically to the universal success of the Great Exhibition of the Work of All Nations in 1851."* These events included pageants and indeed, a large number of pageants were organised in the Festival year. One of these was the 'Three Towns Pageant' organised by the boroughs of Kingston, Richmond and Twickenham. It was held in the grounds of Hampton Court at the back of the palace and ran nightly from 14 to 28 July. The pageant that resulted was one of the largest held during the Festival of Britain. It was on a monumental scale and, it is said, involved 2500 performers from amateur dramatic and operatic companies in the three boroughs. Much of the pageant was based on historical scenes from the area's past although the final scene provided *"a glimpse of some of the activities of the Boroughs to-day"*.

Some Hampton children also went to the actual Festival in London, recorded in the school log book for Hampton Junior School as: *"Jul*

11 The Headmaster and Miss Clark took 22 boys and girls to the South Bank Exhibition of the Festival of Britain. All the children were from Class I. Jul 12 (Further 22 children to Exhibition)".

The third event, of huge national significance and with local celebrations, was the coronation of Queen Elizabeth II on 2 June 1953. She had ascended to the throne on 6 February 1952 after the death of her father, King George VI and is now the longest reigning British monarch. On such a major occasion there were huge celebrations throughout the land.

In Hampton, there was a variety of events held over several weeks. An embroidery and needlework exhibition took place at the Congregational Hall in High Street, Hampton Hill, from 12 to 16 May with over 1000 exhibits. On 30 May a horse show and gymkhana was held in the grounds of *Beveree* (now Twickenham Preparatory School) in High Street, Hampton, from 12.30 until 6pm, with cash and trophy prizes. In the evening of the same day, from 7pm to dusk, there was an Elizabethan water pageant at Bell Hill, near the ferry, where, it was estimated, there were 150 people in costume. There were also strolling minstrels, dancing bears, fencing contests and tilting contests in punts. On 1 June there was a concert for old folks in the Public Hall in Church Street. The following day was the actual Coronation Day and, in the same venue, the old folks were able to watch the Coronation ceremony on television. As television was still in its infancy this would probably have been the first time many people would have seen a TV broadcast. On 3 June there was a Coronation sport event in Bushy Park, including a cricket match, comic football match and a boxing tournament. Then, on 6 June there was the largest local event which was a grand carnival procession starting from Wensleydale Road at 2.30pm proceeding to Hampton Hill and Bushy Park. Entries for the procession were invited in various sections: Tableaux, Decorated Heavy and Light Motor Vehicles, Decorated Motor Cars and Motor Cycles, Decorated Horse-drawn Vehicles, Decorated Pedal Cycles, Mounted Fancy Dress, Fancy Costumes-Adults and Fancy Costumes-Juniors. This was followed, in Bushy Park, by children's sports, presentation of the prizes for the sports and for the various sections of the carnival procession, and a miniature tattoo (military display) put on by local cadets of the armed services. No doubt the grand carnival procession was an event that lived long in the memory of those who witnessed it.

A number of Hampton children also went to see the aftermath of the actual Coronation. The school log book for Hampton Junior School for 8 June 8 says *"This afternoon the school was closed. The children were taken by their teachers on a coach tour of London to see the Coronation decorations"*. The following two days record *"Jun 9 Three playground seats have been purchased as a Coronation gift to the children. Jun 10 This morning all the children with their teachers visited the Savoy Cinema, Teddington, to see the Coronation Film "Elizabeth is Queen"*.

Hampton Ferry

The ferry from Hampton across to Molesey (Hurst Park) has run for over 500 years as it was known to be in existence in 1519 when Henry VIII was on the throne. Our narrative is principally concerned with the 1940s, 1950 & 1960s and so we will look at it through the eyes of someone who started work at the ferry just before WW2. He was Charlie (also known as "Joe") Baker of High Street, Hampton, who died on 12 Mar 2010. He was the last ferryman to regularly row the Hampton Ferry (it has been motorised since 1996).

Charlie, who was born in Hampton, started at the ferry at the age of 12 in 1938. The ferry was then run by Jubilee Waldock, and George Kenton was employed as boatman there. Later, George Kenton took over the business and subsequently became a Hampton Councillor for many years and was later Mayor of the LBRUT. After George Kenton took over the business he would not row the ferry anymore and so Charlie became the ferryman. When he was 18 he enlisted in the Army and joined the Royal Engineers for the end of the war and afterwards and served for three years from 1945-48.

The ferry business did not just involve the ferry but also included a boatyard. In earlier times boats had been built there but by this time only boat repairs were carried out and no actual boats were built during Charlie's time. There would, however, have been a considerable amount of repair and maintenance work as it is known from a 1943 boat registration plate that there were 68 hire boats at the yard at that time.

It is difficult now to envisage how busy the Hampton ferry once was. In the 19th Century, Molesey Hurst, to which the ferry crossed on the Surrey bank, was the scene of the old Hampton Races and also of boxing prize-fights and large numbers crossed the river by ferry. In the late 1880s the old Hampton race course was closed down and a new course with vastly improved facilities known as Hurst Park was built and opened in 1890. Both before and after WW2 the ferry was still very busy, particularly on race days. At the time there were two ferry boats used on Sundays, three ferry boats for Molesey Regatta and no less than seven boats on Hurst Park race days. Of these seven boats Charlie recalled them as being one "flat", four iron boats, one wooden boat and another boat that had possibly been a coal or coke barge for Thornycroft's on nearby Platt's Eyot. The "flat" was a very large flat-bottomed boat that was "poled" across with an 18 ft pole (the river is up to about 11 ft deep at this point). The flat took three men to man it and could carry about 100 passengers at a time. Altogether it took 13 men to run the ferry on race days including people on each side to take the money. The ferry used to carry about 6000 people (3000 each way) on race days. Apparently, the queues on the Hampton side used to stretch back to Barnes alley (off Thames Street and opposite Church Street) to the ferry – a distance of about 300 yards but the queues moved quickly through the turnstiles. The money was apparently collected in large tins which had to be emptied half way through the day and the money hidden. Working hours on race days were 7am to 10pm.

All this changed in 1962 with the closure of Hurst Park race course and the subsequent building of the housing estate on Molesey Hurst. The ferry business fell away and only a single rowing boat was used in latter years. The ferry continued to be rowed until the lease expired in 1995. At this point the ferry owners changed and it was re-launched in 1996 using a motorised ferry. Charlie, although no longer working on the ferry, was not idle and started working on the trip boats from Richmond to Hampton Court during the summer months. He continued to work on the boats until 2008 when he was in his early 80s. He subsequently became ill and spent the last few months of his life in the Star & Garter to which he was entitled as a result of his wartime service. He died at the age of 83 on 12 Mar 2010 – the irony being that he had originally been put to work at the ferry over 70 years before as he had a weak chest and it was thought the fresh air might improve his health. This remedy obviously worked!

The Casino Hotel (originally The Karsino), Tagg's Island

The Karsino was an hotel and entertainment complex on Tagg's Island at Hampton, built by Fred Karno the theatrical impresario, which opened in 1913. The piece de resistance of the hotel was the Palm Court, which was large enough to seat 350 people with a maple dancing floor under an extensive dome painted with riverside scenes.

The complex was never the same after WWI and after a series of bad summers Fred Karno went bankrupt in 1926. The Karsino was taken over by a new owner who spent a considerable outlay on new attractions and re-opened in 1928 as 'The Thames Riviera'. Again, the venture was not successful and was being advertised for sale by 1932. Later it became the 'Palm Beach' and then 'The Casino'. During WW2 the magnificent skating rink and covered tennis courts were converted to a munitions factory and a bridge was built. The Casino hotel was still used for functions in the 1950s and 1960s and dinner dances, where companies would entertain their employees, and similar events were held. The island was put up for sale in 1963 and a new tenant established an exclusive gambling club there in 1965. Various planning applications were then put forward under subsequent owners and the hotel was finally demolished in 1971. After a number of failed planning application, a new bridge was constructed in the early 1980s and the site of the Casino/Karsino was excavated to build a lagoon in the centre of the island for mooring further houseboats. Today houseboats occupy the central lagoon as well as still ringing the island.

Above: A VE (Victory in Europe) Day party in May 1945 in Orchard Road.

HAMPTONS
VICTORY CELEBRATIONS

At the request of the Borough Council, your Hospital Appeals Committee consented to organise on your behalf, the Victory Celebrations. We trust that the programme, although chiefly for children, will attract and interest everyone.

Sunday, June 9th, 1946
CARLISLE PARK, 3 p.m.
Victory Drumhead Service
(The Mayor and Corporation will attend.)

Monday, June 10th, 1946
OFFICIAL OPENING 3 p.m
By His Worship the Mayor.

Children's Sports 3.10 p.m.

In Denmead School Ground
(Loaned with kind permission by W. D. James, Esq.)

Entries on Ground.   *Large number Prizes.*

Each child issued with a Voucher by the School Authorities will on presenting this at Carlisle Park, receive a book of tickets, which will enable them to obtain :—1 Bun, 1 Mineral, 2 Ice Creams, 1 Flag, and entry to view Model of famous Warship, Free of charge.

Free Punch & Judy Shows - Donkey Rides

INTERVAL 6.30—7.30 p.m.

7.30 p.m.   Parade of Hamptons Hospital May Queen and her Maids of Honour.
Followed by DANCING till 10.30 p.m.

DISPLAY OF FIREWORKS - 9.30 p.m.
Grounds Illuminated.   Refreshments obtainable.
Music by Melford Radio.

Meanwhile support your Hospital Memorial Fund.

Left: A poster for Hampton's Victory Celebrations organised as part of the official London Victory Celebrations of 1946.

Below: As part of the 1951 Festival of Britain local pageants were held including the 'Three Towns Pageant' organised by the boroughs of Kingston, Richmond and Twickenham in the grounds of Hampton Court Palace.

Above: As part of the 1953 Coronation celebrations an Elizabethan water pageant was held at Bell Hill, near the ferry, including strolling minstrels, dancing bears, fencing contests and tilting contests in punts.

Right: Another part of the Coronation celebrations was a Coronation Sport event in Bushy Park, including a cricket match, comic football match and a boxing tournament.

A HAMPTON'S CORONATION EVENT

Elizabeth R 1953

Coronation

Sports

On Wednesday, June 3rd. 1953

FOOTBALL — BOXING

Programme—Price 6d.

BUSHY PARK
(HAMPTON HILL ENTRANCE)

6.30 p.m. to 9.00 p.m.

Above: This decorated vehicle won first prize in its category in the Hampton & District Coronation procession on 6 June 1953.

Below: The big freeze of December 1962/January 1963 caused the river to completely freeze over as shown in this view of what would normally be the route crossed by the ferry.

THE THAMES HAMPTON 9.

Above: The Hampton Ferry boatshed (to the left of the boat) in a c1950 postcard.

Below: The Hampton Ferry landing point (a pair of railings on the right) in a c1950 postcard view of Hampton riverside taken from the Molesey bank.

THE THAMES HAMPTON 1.

133

Left: George Kenton, owner of the Hampton Ferry holds up an old charges board used by the ferry.

The board reads:

HAMPTON FERRY

Authorised charges for Passengers single journey
on days other than Hurst Park Race days   2⁺
on Hurst Park Race days ordinary passengers   6ᵈ
Ditto Racing Staff   3ᵈ
Workmens fares (if weekly Tickets are taken)   1⁺
The ordinary ferrying hours are from 6a.m to 10p.m
during the period of British Summer time and
from 6a.m to 8p.m during the remainder of the year
Charges for Vehicles—
For a pedal bicycle a sum equal to the fare
payable by the accompanying passenger.

For a motor cycle 6ᵈ⎫
For a motor car   1⁻⎬ double charges
For a horse & cart 1⁻⎭ on race days

Below: The ferry being rowed by Charlie Baker in a c1965 view with the Hampton riverside in the background.

THE BALLROOM

Above: The Palm Court ballroom at the Casino Hotel could seat 350 people with a maple dancing floor under an extensive dome painted with riverside scenes.

Below: The front of the Casino Hotel advertising *"Dinner Dance on Wednesday, Thursday & Saturday"* in a c1950 view.

FRONT OF THE HOTEL

MAIN SOURCES

50" OS Maps, numerous sheets covering the whole of Hampton of various dates in the 1950s, 1960s & 1970s.

6" OS Map 1938 provisional edition.

5" OS Map 1941 provisional edition with ARP revisions, reduced from the 6" map (London, Sheet 53/18 S.E. (B)).

1940 Kelly's Twickenham, Teddington and Neighbourhood Directory.

1953 Burt's Directory of Twickenham including Teddington, Hampton, Hampton Wick and Whitton.

Numerous Trade and other Directories (particularly those held at Local Studies, Old Town Hall, Richmond and Local Studies, North Kingston Centre).

Numerous Telephone and Business Directories (particularly Yellow Pages and Thomson's).

1969/70 Kingston, Richmond & Twickenham Green Guide.

Electoral Registers for the years between 1939 and 1970. NB (Due to the war there are no registers from 1940 up to 1945).

Building Plan files for numerous properties in Hampton (Local Studies, Old Town Hall, Richmond).

Hampton UDC Street Re-numbering Register (held at Local Studies, Old Town Hall, Richmond).

Map of Borough of Twickenham (War Damage Act, 1941) dated October 1941, colour coded with properties destroyed and damaged (held at Local Studies, Old Town Hall, Richmond).

Verbal information from Charlie Baker, Peter Heath, John Mason and Peter Sait.

Extracts from letters written by Mrs Faith Buckley to her daughters, Janice and June, who had been evacuated to Canada (originally published, in eleven parts, in BOTLHS Newsletters No's 146 – 156, December 2007 – April 2011).

Extracts from the diaries of Mary Grimes formerly of 72 High Street, Hampton (transcribed and extracted by the author from diaries in his possession).

Borough of Twickenham Notes on Invasion Defence No 1 by W H Jones, 1 March 1943.

Extract from article by Raymond Manning "Orme House, 4 Church Street, Hampton & Bushy Park in the 1940s", BOTLHS Newsletter No 164, December 2013.

Looking Backward and Looking Forward to the future Twickenham, brochure to the accompany exhibition at the Municipal Offices, Twickenham, 11 to 22 March, 1946.

The History of Tagg's Island by James Williams, undated.

A Chronicle of Hampton 1956-1981 by G D Heath, Hampton Residents Association, 1981.

100 Years of Specialised Shipbuilding and Engineering (John I Thornycroft Centenary 1964) by K C Barnaby.

Garside's Wars, Memoirs of Bernard Garside F.R.Hist.S. (1898-1963) edited by K A Rice, Published by Hampton School, 1993.

St Albans, Hampton by A F Kelsall (BOTLHS 25), 1972.

Old Hampton, Hampton Hill and Hampton Wick, compiled by members of BOTLHS, Hendon Publishing, 1982.

Hampton in the Nineteenth Century by Gerald Heath (BOTLHS 27), 1993, 2nd edition.

Edwardian Hampton – The Story of Hampton and Hampton Hill from 1900-1914 by John Sheaf (BOTLHS 76), 1997.

When the Bombs Fell by Paul Barnfield (BOTLHS 80), 2001.

Hampton 1915-1937 - The Story of Hampton from the First World War to the Amalgamation with the Borough of Twickenham by John Sheaf (BOTLHS 86), 2005.

The Highways and Byways of Hampton – A short history of every street in Hampton by John Sheaf (BOTLHS 88), 2009.

The Changing Face of Station Road, Hampton – Developments in the Area since the 1860s and a Short History of Every Building in Station Road by John Sheaf (BOTLHS 93), 2014.

Hampton 100 Years Ago – A Description of the Roads and Buildings in 1911 – 1912 by John Sheaf (BOTLHS 95), 2015.

Images of Hampton in the 1920s and 1930s – The Roads and buildings, Businesses and shops, the River and Recreation by John Sheaf (BOTLHS 100), 2017.

ACKNOWLEDGEMENTS

F IRST AND FOREMOST to the late Gerald Heath for his unstinting help and for all the information and material that he kindly gave me, and also to Joan Heath who has also been extremely generous with further help and material.

I would also like to thank members of the Publications Sub-Committee of the Borough of Twickenham Local History Society and particularly those who commented on earlier drafts – Mike Cherry, Chris French and Ed Harris.

Also thanks are due to Jane Baxter and Janine Stanford at the Local Studies Collection, Old Town Hall, Richmond, for their ever helpful attitude and assistance. The photographs are mainly from the collection of the author although the photographs of building plans and several of the photographs are reproduced with the kind permission of the Local Studies Collection, Richmond. I am very grateful to Peter Sait for permission to use the photo of the 'pre-fab' in Oldfield Road.

I am as ever indebted to my wife, Sharman, who helped in numerous ways towards the production of this book

John Sheaf

OTHER BOOKS ABOUT HAMPTON BY JOHN SHEAF

 **EDWARDIAN HAMPTON** - The story of Hampton and Hampton Hill from 1900-1914
BOTLHS Paper 76, 1997

 **HAMPTON 1915-1937** - The story of Hampton from the First World War to the amalgamation with the Borough of Twickenham
BOTLHS Paper 86, 2005

 THE HIGHWAYS AND BYWAYS OF HAMPTON - A short history of every street in Hampton
BOTLHS Paper 88, 2009

 THE CHANGING FACE OF STATION ROAD, HAMPTON - Developments in the area since the 1860s and a short history of every building in Station Road
BOTLHS Paper 93, 2014

HAMPTON 100 YEARS AGO - A description of the roads and buildings in 1911-1912
BOTLHS Paper 95, 2015

 **IMAGES OF HAMPTON IN THE 1920S AND 1930S** - The roads and buildings, businesses and shops, the river and recreation
BOTLHS Paper, 2017

To order any of these publications, please visit www.botlhs.co.uk